Serving New York

For All The People
Who Make NYC Dining
Unforgettable.

Kristin Tice Studeman & Bryan Fountain

Copyright © 2020 by **Kristin Tice Studeman**
Illustrations © 2020 by **Jordan Awan**.

All rights reserved.
Published in the United States by **Kristin Tice Studeman**.

Library of Congress Cataloging-in-Publications
Data is available upon request.

ISBN 978-0-578-75314-0

Printed in the United States of America.

Book design and art direction by **Bryan Fountain**.
Illustrations by **Jordan Awan**.
Photography by **Chelsie Craig**.
Food styling by **Pearl Jones**.
Prop styling by **Nicole Louie**.

BallPill font donated by **Benoit Bodhuin**.
Apoc font donated by **Blaze Type**.

Third Edition.

100% of the profits from *Serving New York*
go to the **ROAR x Robin** Hood restaurant worker relief fund

For **my mother, Lynn**, who has inspired my love of food, restaurants, and cookbooks for as long as I can remember.

And for **Jake, my husband and best friend**: Thank you for being my biggest champion — and for sampling the 1,023 recipes I tested during quarantine. I'll do the dishes as soon as I finish this book...

And to **every restaurant** I've ever loved, and all the ones I have yet to fall for: Thank you for feeding this city every hour of the day. We miss you and hope to see you all up and running again soon.

Snacks, Dips, & Sips
Page 14

Outlook Good Cocktail, HUNKY DORY
The Clara Bow Cocktail, LLAMA INN
Bacon Cheddar Biscuits, GRAMERCY TAVERN
Chex Mix, TOKYO RECORD BAR
Burrata Dream Toast, AVOCADERIA
Farinata, VIC'S
Focaccia, NICHE NICHE
Muhammara, CELESTINE
Open-Faced Tinned Fish Sandwich, RHODORA
Beet Tahini Dip, SAMESA
Kale-Crab Rangoon, OLMSTED
Grilled Cheese and Shallot Jam, THREE OWLS MARKET

Soups & Salads
Page 40

Gem Salad, JUNE
Spring Pea Vignole, PASQUALE JONES
Farro Salad, CHARLIE BIRD
Chicory Salad, LALOU
Fennel Salad, ALTRO PARADISO
Escarole & Strawberry Salad with Gorgonzola, JOJO

Sides
Page 54

Cauliflower with Pear & Hazelnuts, LOCANDA VERDE / THE DUTCH / BAR PRIMI
Hot-Honey Roasted Carrots, 232 BLEECKER
White Beans & Broth, WEST~BOURNE
Sautéed Beets & Farro, THE SMILE & SMILE TO GO
Butternut Squash Bread Pudding, QUALITY EATS

Mains
Page 66

Kimchi Stew with Rice Cakes & Shredded Pork, **MOMOFUKU**
Frittata di Primavera, **KING**
Broccoli Rabe & Chickpea Pasta, **COOKSHOP**
Korean-Style Rice & Eggs, **GOLDEN DINER**
Khichdi, **INDAY**
Butter Beans, 'Nduja, Leeks & Lemon, **SUNDAY IN BROOKLYN**
Pasta with White Wine Sauce & Spring Vegetables, **THE NOMAD**
Roasted Market Fish with Ginger Scallion Sauce, **NOM WAH NOLITA**
Sweet & Sour Brisket, **GERTIE**
Spaghetto al Pomodoro, **EATALY NEW YORK**
Signature Burger, **VIRGINIA'S**
White Bean & Spinach Stew, **SIMON & THE WHALE**
Pasta e Fagioli, **DON ANGIE**
Mac & Cheese, **DIG INN**
Galbi Bowl, **COTE**
Al's French Toast Anglaise, **CROWN SHY**
Pastrami Potato Hash, **CHARLIE PALMER STEAK**
Cajun Rib Steak, **SMITH & WOLLENSKY**
Indonesian Chicken with Vermicelli Noodles, **WAYAN**

Sweets
Page 106

Olive Oil Cake, **HART'S**
Pecan Sandies, **BOUCHON BAKERY**
Coconut-Jam Bars, **OVENLY**
Salted Caramel Pudding, **JOSEPH LEONARD**
Lemon Ricotta Cake with Whipped Whipped Crème Fraîche, **FAUSTO**
Madeleines, **DANIEL**

Acknowledgements
Page 120

About the Author

Kristin Tice Studeman is a writer, editor, and founder of The Rosé Project, a rosé-paired dinner series. Her work has been featured in *Vogue, The New York Times, Condé Nast Traveler, W Magazine,* and *Real Simple*. A native of San Francisco, she lives in New York City.

Forward

My first restaurant job, at dell'anima in New York City's West Village, coincided with the restaurant's first months of existence. I was still in culinary school at the time, and those months were like a crash course in starting a business and running an operation, all while learning the basic techniques of cooking: the ultimate curriculum in multitasking. The intensity and fluidity of the service and the ingenuity of the kitchen brought out my very best. I learned more from that year than I did at any other schooling or job.

More importantly, I found my people. To me, that's really what we work for: to find those who share our vision for what we hope to create in the world.

You'll never meet more creative, perseverant, generous, and empathetic people than the ones who work in the hospitality industry. This business is not for the faint of heart; it's a calling, something you do because you can't imagine doing anything else or with anyone else. I got my start at a restaurant and I am lucky to now own one, too. I'm fortunate to play my favorite sport with the ultimate team. For the long hours, non-existent holidays, physical endurance, and endless sacrifices, there's a pride in nurturing your community. Restaurants are unique, indelible lighthouses that stand for hope, vibrancy, open arms, and possibility.

We live to say yes. We live to stretch ourselves beyond boundaries and go the extra mile to please our guests. We live to hustle and problem-solve on the fly. We live to make magic and to make your day. We live to take care of others.

And now we need others to care for us.

There are about 30,000 restaurants in New York State, and almost 1 million people who work in them. Most are currently unemployed as a result of the coronavirus pandemic. What's worse, many will not have jobs to return to when the country reopens. With paychecks and benefits lost practically overnight, many of our team members don't know how they will cover their rent, put food on the table, or pay for critical expenses like medications, schooling, and child care.

This cookbook, a collection of more than 45 wonderful recipes from my fellow New York City chefs, is dedicated to every bartender who lent you an ear, every busser who cleared your plates, every line cook who prepped your ingredients, and every host who took your coat. It's for chefs and sommeliers, servers and cleaners. It's for the restaurant workers you see and interact with, and it's for the ones who work behind the scenes in order to make your meal—be it a casual Tuesday dinner or a special-occasion blowout—one to remember.

All profits from this cookbook will go toward a New York City employee relief fund created by Relief Opportunities for All Restaurants (ROAR) and Robin Hood, New York City's largest poverty-fighting organization. The funds will provide critical cash assistance to eligible restaurant workers facing unprecedented economic hardship as a result of COVID-19.

By buying this book, you are helping to save restaurants. More than that, though, you are joining our restaurant family. For that, we thank you, and we look forward to welcoming you back into our dining rooms soon.

-**Camilla Marcus**, founding member of **ROAR** and chef + owner of **west~bourne**

Introduction

In February, my husband and I set out for a celebratory dinner at Gramercy Tavern, Danny Meyer's New York City dining institution. When we got there and gave our name, the hostess said she couldn't find our reservation. But despite the packed house—typical for Friday evenings in the winter season—we were escorted to a corner table.

We were then greeted by a server who reminded us what a great restaurant is all about: warmth and hospitality. Anyone who has ever had the pleasure and privilege of dining at Gramercy Tavern has experienced that sprezzatura in ways small and large, usually in the form of little extras. In our case, that meant a dessert surprise: not only the chocolate pudding we had ordered, but also the cheesecake we had been debating aloud.

When I think back on that meal at Gramercy Tavern, I remember the food, of course—and in particular the to-die-for roasted lamb. But what really stands out in my memory is our server's consummate professionalism and infectious enthusiasm. We all have dining experiences like that—a bartender that goes beyond, a sommelier that pulls out just the right bottle, a server who makes a celebratory dinner unforgettable.

It was only a few weeks later that the coronavirus shook every industry in the country. Practically overnight, nearly all of New York City's 26,000-plus restaurants closed. I can only assume that the server we loved so much lost his job amid the restaurant group's publicly announced layoffs. Millions of other restaurant workers, from head chefs and dishwashers to line cooks and receptionists, have also lost their livelihoods.

What is New York City without its restaurants? They are the lifeblood and the backbone of our vibrant, diverse, exciting metropolis. But right now, their future looks uncertain.

That's why this book exists: to support New York City's finest restaurants and their hard-working teams through one of the most powerful, most unifying languages on Earth: recipes.

Some recipes within these pages were made famous in restaurants themselves and earned praise from passionate diners and food critics alike: Greg Baxtrom's smash-hit crab rangoon from Olmsted, in Brooklyn; Daniel Boulud's madeleines from Daniel, his Upper East Side flagship; and Katie Jackson's olive oil cake from Hart's, a Crown Heights favorite where there's nearly always a wait. Others were developed by chefs in their home kitchens using whatever ingredients happened to be on-hand; for example, butter beans and 'nduja from Jaime Young of Sunday in Brooklyn. That scrappiness is an acute reflection of the current pandemic; after all, hour-long waits at grocery stores don't differentiate between novice cooks and Michelin-starred chefs. But no matter our level of skill and expertise, we can all find solace in home-cooked meals—especially now.

I miss restaurants terribly right about now. What I wouldn't give to walk down the street to visit some of my neighborhood favorites. I've been daydreaming about moseying over to west~bourne for the Sunrise Kingdom breakfast sandwich; enjoying a leisurely lunch of warm carta di musica and ravioli at King; and feasting on razor clams and white Burgundy at Charlie Bird. At some point, I know it'll happen. Now, about that Gramercy Tavern dinner: My husband I later discovered that we made our reservation for the wrong day. But despite our foolish error, we were never made to feel anything less than welcome—a true testament to the magic of restaurants and the people who work at them. This book is for them.

Kristin Tice Studeman

Snacks, Dips, AND Sips

Outlook Good Cocktail

Hunky Dory is committed to sustainability. We're all cooking at home a lot more, and chances are there's a pile of herb scraps and stems starting to build up in your kitchen. This bright and herbaceous cocktail is a great way to nip food waste in the bud, plus it's the perfect cooler to sip on your fire escape in warmer months. Best of all, it's simple: Any spirit is suitable for this drink! We prefer mezcal when we're in the mood for something boozy, and dry vermouth when we're digging something lighter.

Claire Sprouse, HUNKY DORY • *Serves 1*

Ingredients

1 cup hot water

1 cup sugar

1/4 cup fresh herb stems and scraps such as basil, mint, or rosemary

1/4 cup (2 ounces) mezcal, dry vermouth or any spirit you have

1 tablespoon (1/2 ounce) lime juice

Steps

Combine water, sugar, and herbs in a small pot. Cook over low heat, stirring often, until sugar is dissolved, about 5 minutes. Let cool, then strain. Herb syrup will keep, tightly covered in the refrigerator, for about a week.

For one cocktail, combine 1 tablespoon herb syrup, the spirit of your choosing, and lime juice in a pint glass and top with ice. Stir and enjoy.

HUNKY DORY

THE Clara Bow Cocktail

This cocktail was co-created with Jim Kearns for a true New York speakeasy bar called Woodson and Ford. We debuted it again on our Rye House menu. Developed in homage to 1920s actress and "It" girl Clara Bow, the whiskey cocktail takes after her grit and the red hue of her hair. Cocktails like this one inspired some of Llama Inn's signature drinks, including the Senorita Spritz.

Lynnette Marrero, LLAMA INN • *Serves 1*

Ingredients

- 3 tablespoons (1½ ounces) bourbon
- 1½ tablespoons (¾ ounce) lemon juice
- 1 tablespoon (½ ounce) elderflower liqueur or elderflower cordial
- 1 tablespoon (½ ounce) grenadine
- 6 mint leaves, plus mint sprig for serving

Steps

Shake bourbon, lemon juice, elderflower liqueur, grenadine and mint leaves in a shaker with ice. Double strain into a coupe glass. Garnish with a mint leaf.

LLAMA INN

Bacon Cheddar Biscuit

We make these mini biscuits as a snack in the Tavern, but I'll make them anywhere, anytime. Try them for breakfast, split in half and topped with a spoonful of scrambled eggs and melted cheddar. Since the biscuit dough balls can be frozen and then baked straight from the freezer, it's easy to keep some on hand. (You can make them bigger if you'd like: just increase the baking time.) If you have the time, freeze the mixed dry ingredients overnight. When the dough is really cold it is more difficult for gluten to form. Less gluten means softer biscuits. From *The Gramercy Tavern Cookbook* by Mike Anthony.

Mike Anthony, GRAMERCY TAVERN • *Makes 50*

Ingredients

1/2 cup diced slab bacon (about 3 ounces)

2 1/4 cups all-purpose flour

3 3/4 teaspoons baking powder

1 teaspoon Kosher salt

1/8 teaspoon cayenne pepper

3 tablespoons unsalted butter, chilled and cubed, plus 2 tablespoons melted unsalted butter

3/4 cup shredded sharp cheddar cheese (about 4 ounces)

1 1/2 cups heavy cream

Steps

Preheat oven to 425°F.

Cook the bacon over medium-low heat in a medium skillet until the fat is rendered and the bacon is browned but not crunchy, about 6 minutes. Using tongs, transfer the bacon to a paper towel-lined plate to cool.

In a large bowl, mix the flour, baking powder, salt, and cayenne. Add the cubed butter and toss to coat with the flour mixture, then, using your fingertips, flatten the pieces of butter. Flattening the bits of butter to mix them with the flour helps produce a really tender biscuit. Stir in the cooked bacon and the cheese. Add the cream and mix until just combined.

Divide the dough into about 50 tablespoon-sized pieces and shape into balls, taking care not to overwork the dough. Transfer the dough balls to a parchment paper-lined baking sheet. At this stage, you can freeze the dough. Once hard, transfer them to a freezer container and keep frozen for up to 2 weeks. (If baking right away, place the balls on 2 parchment-lined baking sheets about 1-inch apart.)

Bake until golden and cooked through, 10 to 12 minutes (add a few minutes if cooking from frozen). Brush with the melted butter and serve hot or at room temperature.

GRAMERCY TAVERN

Chex Mix

This is a recipe I've had since childhood with a slight twist. My mom, Pam Fabian, would make it every other month or so when we had bacon with breakfast. She would save the bacon fat and then toss it into the chex mix creating a sweet, smokey and savory touch. Her chex mix is infamous. We would try and sneak some before it was finished, almost burning our hands reaching for the still-chewy mix.

Since the restaurant is a Japanese-inspired place, we made a couple additions. We added nori and soy sauce to take the place of the bacon fat. This version is kosher, but it's just as addictive as my mother's. You can choose to use these cereals, but it will also work just as well with gluten-free versions.

Zach Fabian, **TOKYO RECORD BAR** • *Makes 15, 1-cup servings*

Ingredients

- 1/2 (12-ounce) bag Butter Snap pretzels or 1/2 (16-ounce bag) Twisted Pretzel
- 1/2 (8.9-ounce) box Cheerios
- 1/2 (12-ounce) box Rice Chex
- 1/2 (0.8-ounce) pack nori, cut into 1-inch x 1/2-inch strips
- 1/2 (16-ounce) tin cocktail peanuts, optional
- 1 (8-ounce) package unsalted butter, melted
- 1/2 cup soy sauce
- 1 tablespoon celery salt
- 1 tablespoon garlic powder
- 1 1/2 tablespoons onion powder

Steps

Preheat oven to 250°F. Line 2 baking sheets with parchment paper. In an extra large bowl, toss together the pretzels, cereals, nori, and peanuts, if using.

In a medium bowl, whisk together the butter, soy sauce, celery salt, garlic powder, and onion powder. Pour over the pretzel mixture and toss until evenly coated and well combined. Spread into an even layer on prepared baking sheets. Bake, removing from the oven and stirring every 15 minutes, until crisp and fragrant, 1 hour. Set aside to cool completely (mixture will harden once cooled).

TOKYO RECORD BAR

Burrata Dream Toast

We picked this recipe because it's easy and playful, but also very tasty. This is our riff on a beloved Italian springtime bruschetta. Just be careful when taking a bite—the burrata is deliciously messy, so a knife and fork would come in handy here.

Francesco Brachetti & Alessandro Biggi, AVOCADERIA • *Serves 2*

Ingredients

2 sprigs fresh mint, plus more for topping

2 cloves garlic

1 tablespoon olive oil, plus 1 teaspoon for serving

2 cups frozen peas, thawed

½ teaspoon sugar

½ teaspoon fine sea salt

Freshly ground black pepper, to taste

1 piece ciabatta bread (about 5 x 5 inches each), split and toasted

1 avocado, pitted, peeled, and sliced

2 small balls burrata cheese, at room temperature

Pea shoots, for topping, optional

Steps

In a small saucepan, combine mint, garlic, and 1 tablespoon oil and cook over low heat for 30 seconds. Stir in the peas, sugar, salt, and pepper; cook for 5 minutes. Add ¼ cup water and cover; cook until the peas are fork-tender and there's still some liquid in the pan, about 10 minutes. Remove from the heat. Reserve 1 tablespoon of whole peas for topping the toasts. Transfer remaining pea mixture to a food processor and pulse until coarsely mashed. If you don't have a food processor, mash pea mixture with a fork for a slightly chunkier texture. Finished mixture is about 1 cup.

Spread about ½ cup pea spread over each toasted ciabatta bottom. Divide the sliced avocado between the toasts, placing it in the center, and set the burrata ball on top. Scatter over the reserved cooked peas, mint, and pea shoots (if using), then drizzle with olive oil and sprinkle with pepper.

AVOCADERIA

Farinata

Hillary Sterling and Pam Krauss, VIC'S • *Makes one large pancake*

Ingredients

2¼ cups chickpea flour

1 tablespoon kosher salt

4 cups water

4 scallions or ramps, halved crosswise

1 tablespoon olive oil

½ cup mozzarella cheese

½ lemon, for serving

Grated Pecorino Romano or Parmesan, for serving

Black pepper, for serving

Steps

Combine chickpea flour and salt in a bowl. Slowly whisk in water until batter is smooth. Cover with plastic wrap and allow to sit at room temperature for 3 hours. Batter can be made up to 2 days ahead (refrigerate until ready to use).

Preheat oven to 500 °F. Heat a 10- or 12-inch cast iron skillet over high heat. Add scallions and cook, turning occasionally, until blistered, 3 to 5 minutes. Transfer scallions to a plate.

Add olive oil and swirl to coat the bottom of the skillet. Add batter (there should be a very explosive reaction once the batter hits the pan) and lower the heat to medium low. Cook until set around the edge of the pan, about 5 minutes. Once the batter is set, you should start seeing little bubbles on top similar to cooking pancakes.

Transfer skillet to oven and bake until top is pale, golden brown and a toothpick or cake tester inserted into the center comes out clean, 8 minutes. Remove from oven and top with mozzarella and scallions. Return to the oven and cook until the cheese is melted, about 2 minutes. Squeeze lemon over top, sprinkle with Pecorino and finish with cracked pepper. Serve immediately.

VIC'S

Muhammara

Muhammara is a Syrian dip with hot peppers, usually Aleppo peppers. We use jarred piquillos to give a sweet note to the spread as well as dried Aleppo pepper, but you can use jarred roasted red pepper and red pepper flakes in a pinch. Serve with sliced raw vegetables, such as carrots or cucumbers, and/or flatbread.

Garett McMahan, **CELESTINE** • *Makes ¾ cup*

Ingredients

- 1 medium chile pepper, such as fresno or red jalapeno
- 1 cup walnut halves
- ⅓ cup coarsely chopped, rinsed and drained, roasted piquillo or other red peppers (from a jar)
- ¼ cup extra-virgin olive oil, plus more for serving
- 1 medium garlic clove, peeled
- 1¼ teaspoons fresh lemon juice, plus more to taste
- ¼ teaspoon paprika
- Kosher salt
- Walnut oil or olive oil, flaky sea salt, Aleppo pepper or crushed red pepper flakes, and sliced raw vegetables and/or flatbread for serving

Steps

Preheat broiler. Broil chile on a rimmed baking sheet, turning occasionally, until blistered and blackened, 5 to 7 minutes. Remove from oven and let cool 5 minutes, then stem, peel, and seed; set aside.

Preheat oven to 350°F. Toast walnuts on a rimmed baking sheet, stirring halfway through, until golden and fragrant, 8 to 10 minutes. Remove from oven and let cool.

Set aside 2 tablespoons walnuts. In a food processor, combine remaining nuts, reserved chile pepper, roasted piquillo or other red peppers, olive oil, garlic, lemon juice, paprika, and ¾ teaspoon salt. Puree until smooth, add salt, pepper, and lemon juice to taste.

Transfer the muhammara to a serving bowl. Chop and scatter reserved walnuts on top. Drizzle with walnut or olive oil and sprinkle with flaky salt and Aleppo pepper or red pepper flakes. Serve with sliced raw vegetables and/or flatbread.

Muhammara keeps, covered and refrigerated, up to 2 days.

CELESTINE

Open-Faced Tinned Fish Sandwich

This recipe is perfect for a solo snack, or, when doubled, a pre-dinner quarantine snack for a few!

RHODORA • *Serves 1*

Ingredients

- 1 slice of bread from a hearty loaf (rye, sourdough, whatever you have)
- 2 tablespoons crème fraîche, sour cream, or mayo
- 1 4-ounce can tinned fish (smoked trout, sardines, mackerel), drained
- Pickled onions (or pickled anything), for serving
- 2 tablespoons fresh herb leaves, (such as parsley, dill or cilantro), for serving, optional
- Flaky sea salt, for serving

Steps

Toast bread until golden brown and slice in half. Spread 1 tablespoon crème fraîche, sour cream, or mayo on each half. Divide fish between bread pieces. Top with pickled onions, herbs, if using, and flaky sea salt.

RHODORA

Focaccia

This recipe is special to Niche Niche because although we change the menu constantly, this bread is usually on the menu every day in some form or another. Our guests love it and have come to expect it. Work some grilled peppers into the dough, or press roasted garlic cloves into the surface, or grate some cheese over top before you bake it.

Aaron Lirette, NICHE NICHE • *Makes one half sheet tray*

Ingredients

1 ¼-ounce packet (about 2¼ teaspoons) active dry yeast

1 tablespoons extra-virgin olive oil, plus more for the the bowl, baking sheet, and drizzling the top

9⅔ cups all-purpose flour

2 tablespoons plus 2 teaspoons Diamond Crystal Kosher salt

1 tablespoon Maldon salt

1 tablespoon fresh rosemary leaves

Steps

In the bowl of a stand mixer fitted with the dough hook, combine the yeast and 1 tablespoon olive oil, then whisk in 4¼ cups room temperature water. Add the flour and Kosher salt and mix on low to incorporate. When all the flour has been moistened, increase the speed to medium high and continue to mix, scraping down the sides of the bowl with a bench scraper once, until the dough is smooth but still sticky, elastic, and gathered around the dough hook, 10 to 12 minutes (it will seem very wet, which is normal).

Generously oil a separate large bowl. Scrape the dough into the bowl and cover. Let the bowl sit in a warm spot until the dough has doubled in size, 60 to 75 minutes.

Meanwhile, generously oil a half sheet tray and set aside.

Uncover the risen dough and scrape it onto the prepared baking sheet, stretching it into an even layer and into the corners. Drizzle the top with more olive oil. Cover with a sheet of plastic and let sit at room temperature until it's risen, 30 to 45 minutes.

Meanwhile, arrange an oven rack in the center position and preheat oven to 500°F or as high as it will go.

Uncover the dough. Oil hands and press fingertips into dough, pushing down to the bottom of the pan to dimple all over. Sprinkle with Maldon salt and rosemary. Transfer to the oven and bake until deep golden brown, rotating the pan 180° halfway through, 20 to 25 minutes.

Remove the focaccia from the oven and let cool for 10 minutes in the sheet tray. Slide a thin metal spatula around the sides of the focaccia and underneath, to loosen. Let cool completely and then cut into pieces and serve.

NICHE NICHE

Beet Tahini Dip

Our garlicky beet dip has been on the menu from the very beginning. When we started Samesa as a pop-up in Brooklyn in 2015, this vibrant hued tahini was an instant hit and remains wildly popular today. It also happens to be a perfect quarantine recipe, since it's super easy to make and requires only a few ingredients. Serve it with pita, crackers, or raw vegetables, or slather it on toasted bread as part of your favorite sandwich.

Eli Sussman, **SAMESA** • *Serves 8 to 10*

Ingredients

- 1½ pounds red beets (2 to 3 large beets), scrubbed
- 1 clove garlic, chopped
- 2 teaspoons olive oil, divided
- 1 teaspoon ground coriander
- ¾ teaspoon ground cumin
- 1 teaspoon Kosher salt
- 1 tablespoon lemon juice
- ¼ cup plus 2 tablespoons well-stirred tahini paste
- Pita chips and fresh cut veggies, for serving

Steps

Bring a large pot of water to boil. Add beets and cook until tender (a knife slides in and out easily), 40 to 55 minutes, depending on the size of the beets.

Remove beets from water and let cool slightly. Rub the skins off with a paper towel. Transfer to the refrigerator to cool completely, about 30 minutes.

Once cool, roughly chop beets into 1-inch pieces. Add garlic, half of beets, and 1 teaspoon of the olive oil to a high-speed blender and blend on high until smooth, 2 minutes. If the mixture is too thick to blend, add half of the lemon juice.

Add coriander, cumin, salt, and remaining beets and blend until smooth, 1 minute more. With the blender running, add lemon juice until incorporated, followed by remaining 1 teaspoon olive oil. Continue blending until oil is fully incorporated. Taste and season with more coriander, cumin, or salt, if desired.

Transfer dip to a large mixing bowl. Add tahini and stir until fully incorporated. Cover with plastic wrap or transfer to an airtight container and chill in refrigerator 1 hour before serving.

Serve with pita chips and/or fresh cut veggies.

SANNESA

Kale-Crab Rangoon

Greg Baxtrom, OLMSTED • *Makes about 30 wontons*

Ingredients

1 tablespoon olive oil

1 cup curly kale, stems removed, leaves finely chopped

Kosher salt, to taste

1 cup fresh ricotta cheese, chilled

1 cup picked crab meat, chilled

30 fresh or frozen square wonton wrappers (from 1 12-ounce package)

1 quart neutral oil, such as canola or vegetable, for frying

Ponzu, sriracha mayo, sweet chile sauce, or hot sauce, for serving

Steps

Heat olive oil in a saucepan or skillet over medium heat. Add kale, season with a pinch of salt, and cook until wilted but still bright green, 3 to 4 minutes. Transfer kale to a medium bowl to cool completely, then stir in the chilled ricotta and crab meat. Season filling with salt to taste.

Place about 10 wonton wrappers on a clean, dry surface. (If using frozen wonton wrappers, defrost for about 40 minutes under damp towel at room temperature or overnight in the refrigerator before shaping.) Cover remaining wonton wrappers under a damp towel, which will prevent them from drying out as you fill the wontons. Place a heaped teaspoon of filling onto the center of each wrapper, leaving the edges clean. (The goal is to fill the wrapper with ample filling while ensuring that the edges stay clean so they can be sealed tightly.)

Fill a small bowl with water, dip your index finger in water and trace the edges of the first wrapper. Bring two opposite corners together in the middle of the wonton and pinch. Repeat with the other two corners and pinch to form a package shape. Then follow the seams down toward the filling, pressing and sealing as you work, expelling any air pockets. Repeat sealing process with the water and remaining filled wrappers. Set aside.

Alternatively, for a simpler fold, pull one corner over and connect it to the opposite corner, forming a triangle. Gently flatten the edges around the filling with your fingers to expel any air pockets and press to seal. In two batches, repeat filling and sealing process with remaining wrappers until no more filling remains.

To deep fry the wontons, heat vegetable oil in a medium pot over high heat to 350°F, as registered on an instant-read thermometer, about 3 to 5 minutes. In 6 batches and carefully adding one wonton at a time, fry wontons in hot oil until crisp and golden brown, about 3 minutes. The wontons should be completely submerged and should bubble immediately when dropped into the oil. Transfer to a baking sheet and keep warm in oven at 200°F until ready to serve. If oil is getting too hot reduce heat to medium-high.

Serve wontons immediately with desired sauce.

OLMSTED

Grilled Cheese AND Shallot Jam

I would say this mashup of melted cheese and caramelized shallot jam is peak grilled cheese perfection. At Three Owls we use a mix of Gruyère and Cheddar cheese, but you can pick whatever meltable cheese you want and any bread you have. I like to throw a little vermouth (my second favorite ingredient after shallots) in the jam, and then use the shallot jam on everything from roasted chicken to scrambled eggs.

Suzanne Dumaine, **THREE OWLS MARKET** • *Serves 1*

Ingredients

- 2 tablespoons unsalted butter
- 3 large shallots, peeled and sliced crosswise into thin rings (about 1½ cups sliced)
- 1½ teaspoons fresh thyme, or ½ teaspoon dried thyme, optional
- Kosher salt
- 2 teaspoons white wine vinegar, Champagne vinegar, or red wine vinegar
- Splash of dry, white vermouth, optional
- 2 tablespoons mayonnaise, divided
- 2 slices bread (marbled rye, wheat, white, challah...)
- ¼ cup grated Gruyère cheese (about 1 ounce)
- ¼ cup grated Cheddar cheese (about 1 ounce)
- Flaky sea salt, for serving

Steps

Melt butter in a small frying pan or saucepan over medium heat. Add shallots and thyme, and season lightly with salt. Cook, stirring often, until shallots begin to soften and the bottom of the pot is almost dry, about 5 to 6 minutes. Add a splash of water (about a tablespoon). Continue stirring shallots occasionally, adding a splash of water every time the bottom of the pot gets dry and looks like it has burnt bits, scraping the bottom of the pan and stirring to incorporate. Continue until the shallots are soft, deeply colored and caramelized, about 20 to 25 minutes. Add vinegar and vermouth, scraping and stirring to pick up the brown bits on the bottom of the pan. Stir until liquid is fully absorbed, about 1 to 2 minutes. Remove from the heat.

Heat a nonstick pan over medium heat. Spread 1 tablespoon of mayonnaise on one side of one slice of bread and place it mayo-side down in the pan. (You do not need to add anything to the pan, the mayo is sufficient.) Combine the cheese together in a small bowl and pile on top of the bread in an even layer. Slather one side of the second piece of bread with remaining tablespoon of mayonnaise. On the other side, spread about a tablespoon of shallot jam and place face down (mayo side up) on top of the melting cheese.

Cook until bread on the bottom side is golden brown, about 3 to 4 minutes. Flip and continue cooking, pressing down with a spatula, until the second side is golden brown and cheese is melted, about 2 to 3 minutes more.

Slice on a diagonal, sprinkle with sea salt and eat promptly.

THREE OWLS MARKET

Soups AND Salads

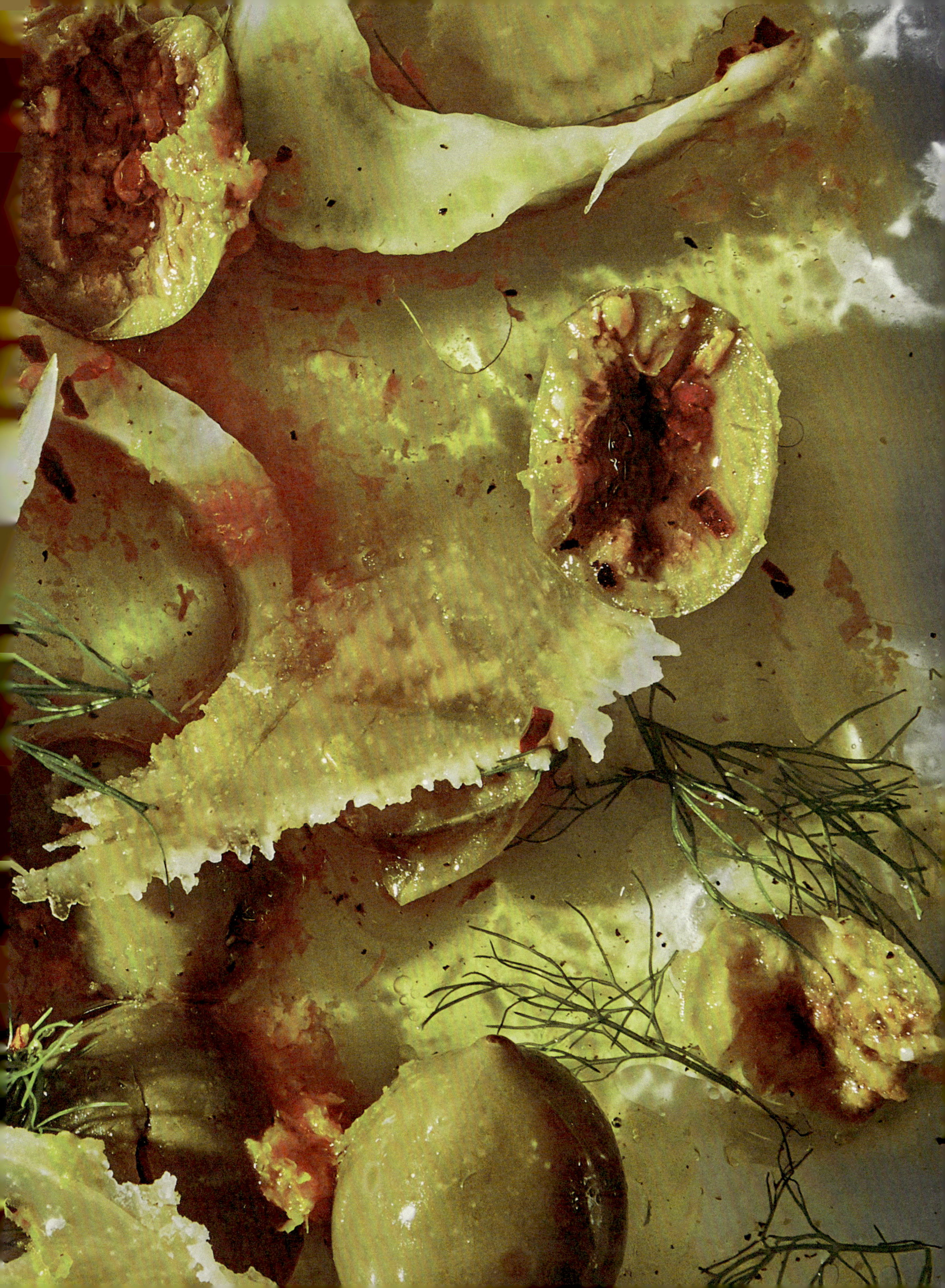

Gem Salad

Tom Kearney, JUNE • *Serves 4*

Ingredients

¼ cup buttermilk

¼ cup crème fraîche or sour cream

¼ cup mayonnaise

½ teaspoon lemon zest plus 1½ teaspoons lemon juice

Coarsely ground black pepper

¼ teaspoon onion powder

Kosher salt

4 heads little gem or butter lettuce

8 breakfast or other radishes, sliced

2 tablespoons chopped fresh herbs such as dill, tarragon, parsley, and/or chives

2 cups frozen peas or frozen sprouted mung beans, thawed

1 cup toasted seeds such as sunflower, chia, flax, or sesame

Steps

Whisk together buttermilk, crème fraîche, mayonnaise, lemon zest, lemon juice, black pepper, onion powder, and ¼ teaspoon salt in a large bowl. Add lettuce, radishes, herbs, and pinch salt, and toss gently to combine.

Divide salad among plates. Garnish with peas or mung beans, and seeds.

JUNE

Spring Pea Vignole

The dish is a collection of all of the greatest things coming out of the garden. It's flavorful and reminiscent of my favorite season—spring.

Ryan Hardy, **PASQUALE JONES** • *Serves 4 to 6*

Ingredients

- ½ cup pancetta or thick-cut bacon, diced into ½-inch pieces
- 1½ cups extra-virgin olive oil, divided
- 1 small head fennel, finely diced
- 1 small yellow onion, finely diced
- 1 whole carrot, finely diced or ground in food processor
- 3 spring onions or scallions, peeled and thinly sliced
- 1 14-ounce can whole artichoke hearts, coarsely chopped
- 3 garlic cloves, peeled and minced
- 2 cups dry white wine
- 3 cups spring peas, fresh or frozen
- 2 cups fava beans, freshly podded, optional
- 1 Parmesan rind, approximately 4x4 inch chunk
- 3½ teaspoons sea salt, plus more to taste
- 2 teaspoons freshly ground black pepper
- ¼ cup fresh mint, chopped
- ¼ cup fresh parsley, chopped

Steps

In a large, straight-sided sauté pan, render the pancetta over medium-heat until golden and crispy, 6 minutes. Using a slotted spoon, transfer the pancetta to a paper towel-lined plate and set aside.

Add 1 cup olive oil to pan, along with fennel, onion, carrot, and spring onions. Cook, stirring occasionally, until soft and translucent, about 20 minutes, then stir in artichokes and garlic. Cook 5 minutes more, then stir in wine. Cook until wine has mostly evaporated, 11 minutes. Stir in peas, fava beans (if using), and Parmesan rind. Season with salt and pepper and cover with 4 cups water. Bring to a simmer over medium-low and cook vegetables are tender, 16 minutes. Remove from heat and let the vignole rest for 15 minutes or up to 2 hours for flavors to blend.

Reheat vignole 10 minutes over medium heat. Remove Parmesan rind. Stir in the mint and parsley. Season with salt and serve warm, topped with reserved crispy pancetta.

PASQUALE JONES

Farro Salad

Farro might be considered a trendy grain now, but it was even trendier about two thousand years ago in Rome, where it was prized for supposedly increasing stamina in the bedroom. We loved that idea, so we knew we had to work it into the menu from day one. The resulting salad is the perfect blend of freshness, texture and goodies (tomatoes, basil, and Parmigiano cheese) to make anyone smile—in the bedroom or elsewhere! If you don't have tomatoes, substitute something seasonal—roasted pumpkin and fennel in the fall, fava beans and char-grilled spring onions in the spring—or use whatever you have at home.

Ryan Hardy, CHARLIE BIRD • *Serves 2 to 4*

Ingredients

1 cup farro

½ cup apple cider

2 cups water, plus more if necessary

½ tablespoon Kosher salt

2 bay leaves

½ cup cherry tomatoes, halved

½ cup parmigiano cheese, shaved with a vegetable peeler

½ cup roasted, shelled pistachios

2 tablespoons lemon juice

¼ cup extra-virgin olive oil

½ cup arugula leaves

¼ cup basil leaves, whole

¼ cup mint leaves, whole

6 radishes, thinly sliced

2 teaspoons Maldon sea salt

Freshly ground black pepper, to taste

Steps

Cover farro with apple cider, water, salt, and bay leaves in medium heavy pot and bring to a simmer. Cook covered, adding more water if necessary, until grains are tender and liquid is absorbed, about 30 minutes, draining any excess liquid that remains. Discard bay leaves and let farro cool.

Combine farro, tomatoes, cheese, pistachios, lemon and olive oil in a large bowl and toss to combine. This base can sit at room temperature for up to an hour, or be covered and refrigerated overnight. Just before serving, add the arugula, basil, mint, radishes, and Maldon sea salt and toss to combine. (Waiting to add these til the very end maximizes the crunch and texture of the salad.)

Serve at room temperature or chilled.

CHARLIE BIRD

Chicory Salad

I love that this salad is bitter, sweet, salty, and crunchy. If you can't find radicchio (or don't like its bitterness), look for a hearty green (like kale) that will hold up to the other components. Either way, these leaves can handle a lot of dressing, so be generous.

Jay Wolman, LALOU • *Serves 2*

Ingredients

¼ cup plus 2 tablespoons extra-virgin olive oil

1 lemon, zested and juiced

1 teaspoon honey

Kosher salt

1 head of radicchio, or other hearty green

1 cup of walnuts, toasted

1 pear or apple, thinly sliced

¼ cup (1 ounce) Manchego, Cheddar, or Parmesan cheese, shaved with a vegetable peeler, plus more for garnish

Fresh cracked pepper, to taste

Steps

Combine extra-virgin olive oil, lemon juice and zest, honey, and pinch of salt in a small bowl and whisk together. Set vinaigrette aside.

Cut the bottom core off the radicchio and tear the leaves into bite-sized pieces. Set out plates and layer radicchio, walnuts, pear or apple, and cheese. (There should be one layer of each ingredient.)

To finish, drizzle each salad with 1 to 2 tablespoons of vinaigrette, shave more ribbons of cheese, and top with fresh cracked pepper.

LALOU

Fennel Salad with Castelvetrano Olives and Provolone

Ignacio Mattos, ALTRO PARADISO • *Serves 4*

Ingredients

2 large fennel bulbs, fronds and stems removed and reserved.

1 cup Castelvetrano olives; pitted, crushed, and coarsely chopped

1/4 cup extra-virgin olive oil

2 tablespoons Chardonnay or other white wine vinegar

1 teaspoon finely grated orange zest

Pinch crushed red pepper flakes

Kosher salt

Freshly ground black pepper

1 lemon, zested and juiced (about 1 teaspoon zest and 2 tablespoons juice)

3 ounces aged provolone cheese or Parmesan, shaved with a vegetable peeler (about 1 cup)

Flaky sea salt, for serving

Steps

Remove outer leaves from fennel bulbs, if bruised or brown. Slice fennel stems crosswise into ¼-inch lengths. Coarsely chop fennel fronds, if using, to yield ⅓ cup (none or less is fine, depending on what you have to work with). Combine stems and fronds, if using, in a medium bowl.

Add olives, oil, vinegar, orange zest, and red pepper flakes to bowl with fennel. Season with pinch each kosher salt and black pepper, and toss to coat.

Halve fennel bulbs lengthwise, then, using a sharp chefs knife or adjustable-blade slicer, thinly shave crosswise (slices should be ⅛-inch thick or thinner). In a large bowl, toss together fennel slices, lemon zest, lemon juice, and generous pinch kosher salt. Adjust salt to taste.

Divide olive mixture among plates. Top with cheese, then fennel mixture. Season with flaky sea salt to taste

ALTRO PARADISO

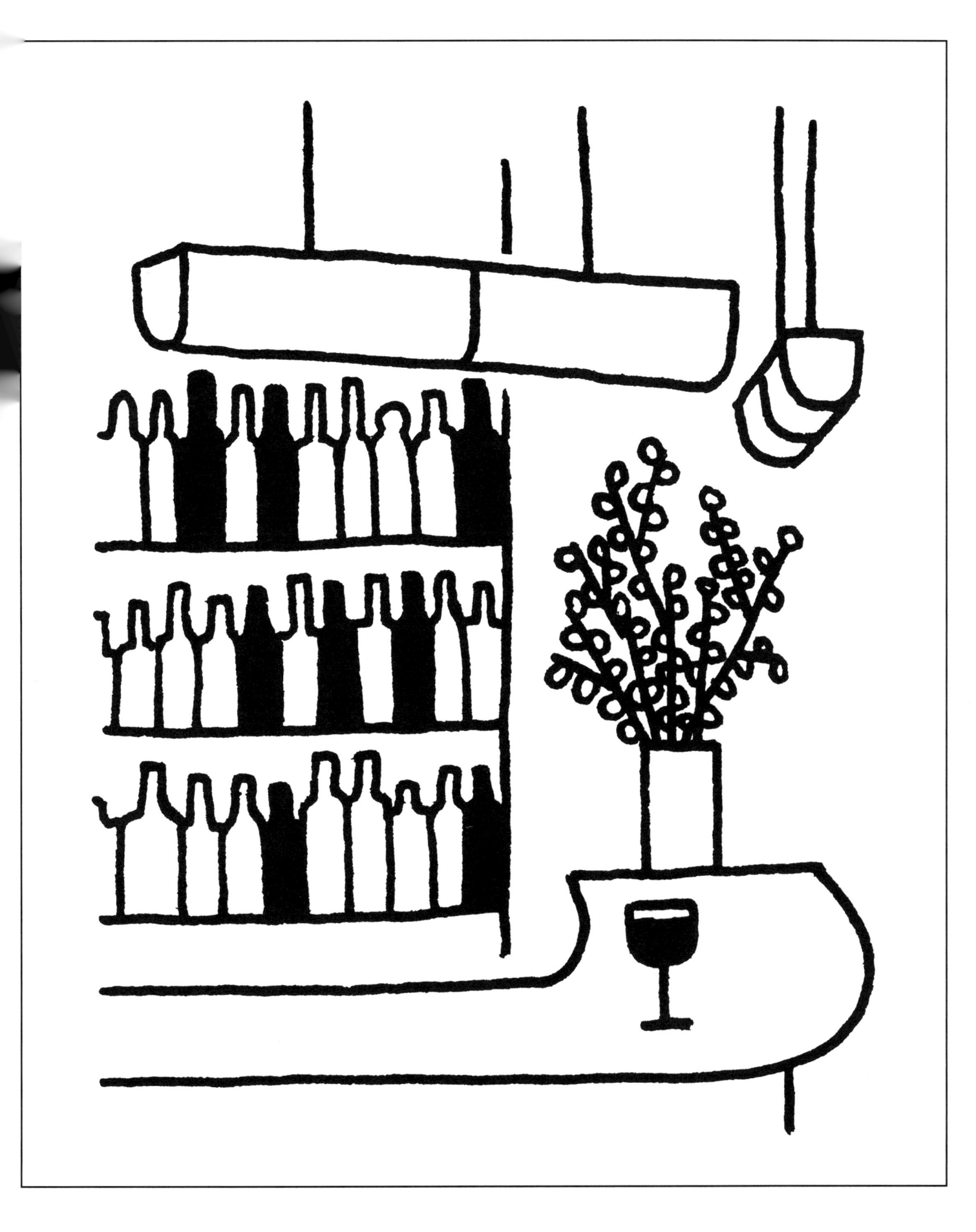

Escarole and Strawberry Salad with Gorgonzola

Jean-Georges Vongerichten, JOJO • *Serves 4*

Ingredients

Dressing

- 3 tablespoons sherry vinegar
- 2 teaspoons fresh lemon juice
- 1/2 teaspoon Kosher salt
- 1/3 cup extra-virgin olive oil, plus more for serving
- 1 teaspoon lemon zest

Salad and Assembly

- 2 cups baby gem lettuce leaves, washed and dried
- 1 cup frisée, endive or radicchio
- 1/2 cup dressing
- 1 cup strawberries (preferably Harry's Berries, if you can find them!), quartered
- 1/2 cup Gorgonzola or other blue cheese, crumbled, at room temperature
- Freshly ground black pepper, for serving
- Fresh basil leaves, torn, for serving

Steps

Dressing: Combine sherry vinegar, lemon juice, salt, olive oil, and lemon zest in a small bowl and whisk to combine. (You will have more dressing than the recipe requires. Cover and chill the rest for later use, up to 1 week.)

Salad and Assembly: Arrange baby gem lettuce, frisée, 2 tablespoons dressing, strawberries, and gorgonzola in even layers on a serving plate. Finish with extra-virgin olive oil, ground black pepper, and basil leaves.

JOJO

Sides

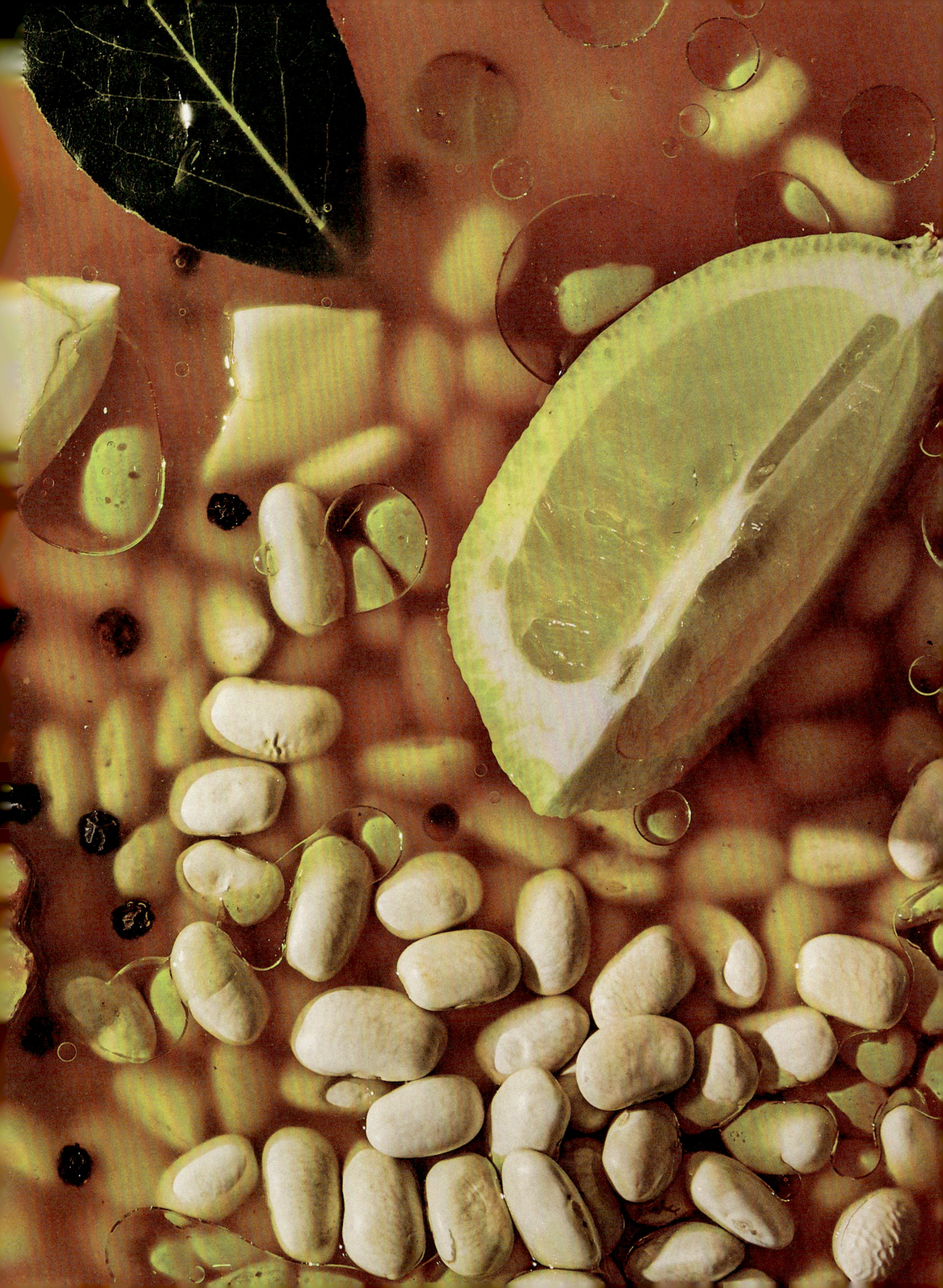

Cauliflower with Hazelnuts and Pear

Andrew Carmellini, LOCANDA VERDE, THE DUTCH, & BAR PRIMI • *Serves 4*

Ingredients

1 cup raw hazelnuts

4 tablespoons unsalted butter

1 medium head cauliflower, greens and stems removed, cut into small florets (about the size of a grape), about 3 cups

8 fresh sage leaves, thinly sliced, about 2 tablespoons

Kosher sea salt

Freshly ground black pepper

1 medium firm-ripe Bosc pears, cored and thinly sliced

1/4 cup fresh flat-leaf parsley leaves, finely chopped

Steps

Finely chop hazelnuts on a cutting board. Heat a heavy-bottomed large skillet over medium heat. Add hazelnuts and cook, shaking the pan occasionally, until lightly toasted, 8 to 10 minutes. Remove from heat and set aside.

Wipe out the skillet and return it to medium-high heat. Add the butter and cook until bubbly and beginning to brown, about 2 minutes. Reduce the heat to medium. Add the cauliflower, sage, and a few generous pinches of salt and pepper and cook, stirring occasionally, until the cauliflower is tender and has browned in spots, 10 to 15 minutes.

Add the pear, parsley, and hazelnuts to the pan and stir to combine. Season with salt and pepper, to taste. Serve warm or at room temperature.

LOCANDA VERDE, THE DUTCH, & BAR PRIMI

Hot–Honey Roasted Carrots

Carrots are one of my favorite vegetables to cook. There are delicious varieties grown most of the year, and they're easy to find in any grocery store. We finish them on our wood-burning grill, but they can be just as tasty right out of a home oven.

Suzanne Cupps, 232 BLEECKER • *Serves 4*

Ingredients

- 8 medium carrots, peeled
- 3 tablespoons extra-virgin olive oil
- Kosher salt
- 1 whole dried Espelette pepper or other variety, such as ancho, chipotle, or guajillo, stem removed
- 1/4 cup honey
- 1 tablespoon water
- Pinch cayenne pepper
- 1/2 lemon
- 1 cup fresh ricotta cheese

Steps

Preheat oven to 400°F.

Arrange carrots on a rimmed baking sheet or in a baking dish. Add oil and 1 teaspoon salt. Toss to combine. Roast, shaking pan halfway through, until carrots are tender (the tip of a small knife should go easily through the root end), 30 to 35 minutes, depending on size.

Meanwhile, combine pepper, honey, and 1 tablespoon water in a small saucepan. Bring to a simmer over low heat, then continue cooking until the pepper softens, about 15 minutes. Keep an eye on the mixture, being careful to not let it boil over or scorch.

Remove honey mixture from heat. Remove and discard dried pepper. Stir in cayenne and 1/2 teaspoon salt. Let cool to room temperature.

Spread ricotta on a serving platter. Arrange carrots on top. Drizzle with honey mixture, then top with a squeeze of lemon, and serve.

Note: To get more of a blackened/charred carrot like we do in the restaurant, you can cook them ahead of time and cool in the fridge. Before serving, I like to cut them in half down the middle and char them (cut side down) in a sauté pan with olive oil. When they have a little color, turn the heat way down, add a small tab of butter, along with the honey and lemon juice, and it'll glaze the carrots nicely.

232 BLEECKER

White Beans and Broth

This hearty, healthy dish was created to help people be less afraid of dried beans. The beans are delicious all on their own, but Camilla Marcus, chef and owner of west~bourne, likes to serve them topped with fennel fritters, mint, labneh, and a drizzle of good olive oil.

Camilla Marcus, WEST~BOURNE • *Serves 4*

Ingredients

2 cups dried cannellini beans

6 cups vegetable stock

¼ cup extra-virgin olive oil, plus more for serving

¼ cup dry white wine

1 lemon, cut into quarters and seeded

2 cloves garlic, gently smashed and peeled

1 tablespoon finely chopped peeled ginger

2 bay leaves

1 tablespoon Kosher salt

6 whole black peppercorns

Fresh mint leaves and flaky sea salt, for serving

Labneh or Greek yogurt, for serving

Steps

Place beans in a large bowl. Add water to cover by 2 to 3 inches. Soak overnight.

Drain and transfer beans to a large pot. Add vegetable stock and enough water to cover by 2 inches. Add oil, wine, lemon quarters, garlic cloves, ginger, bay leaves, salt, and black peppercorns. Bring to a simmer over medium-high heat. Reduce heat to medium-low, cover pot, and simmer, until beans are tender with a little bite, not grainy, and still hold their shape, 1½ to 2 hours.

Remove beans from heat and let cool, covered, for 1 hour.

Remove and discard bay leaves, peppercorns, and lemons. Serve beans warm, with a little of the bean liquid, topped with mint, sea salt, labneh and a drizzle of olive oil.

WEST~BOURNE

Sautéed Beets and Farro

This dish has been on the menu at Smile To Go for years. It's one of my personal favorites and it doesn't rely on super fresh, seasonal produce to make it work. I like to quickly pan-cook the raw beets (skins and all) rather than slow roasting—you get some of the classic beet sweetness but also a nice, firm texture. Fried capers add a salty crunch to balance the beets.

Melia Marden, THE SMILE & SMILE TO GO • *Serves 4*

Ingredients

¼ cup non-pareil capers, drained

1 cup vegetable oil

2 large raw beets (gold, pink, red or whatever you can get, 1 pound total), trimmed and cleaned

4 tablespoons extra-virgin olive oil, divided

Kosher salt, to taste

2 shallots, thinly sliced

Freshly ground black pepper, to taste

2 tablespoons freshly squeezed lemon juice, plus more for serving

6 cooked cups farro or brown rice

½ cup tightly packed, fresh flat-leaf parsley leaves

Steps

Pat capers dry with a paper towel. Heat vegetable oil in a medium skillet or saucepan over high heat until a caper sizzles when dropped in oil. Carefully add capers (oil will sputter) and cook until capers open up and crisp, 2 to 3 minutes. Remove with a slotted spoon and drain on a paper-towel lined plate. Set aside. Let oil cool completely. To re-use, strain through a fine mesh sieve or a double layer of cheesecloth and store in an airtight container.

Slice the beets into thin (⅛-inch) rounds (a mandolin is best, but a sharp chef's knife will work). Toss the beets with 1 tablespoon olive oil and a pinch of salt in a large bowl and let sit until softened slightly, 10 minutes.

Heat remaining 3 tablespoons olive oil in a large skillet over medium heat. Add the shallots and a pinch of salt and cook, stirring occasionally, until softened but not browned, 2 to 3 minutes. Add the beets and season with ½ teaspoon salt and several grinds of pepper. Cook over medium-high heat, stirring often, until the beets are soft, about 5 minutes. Add the lemon juice and cook for 1 minute more. Remove from heat.

Transfer beet mixture to the large bowl. Add farro, parsley, and fried capers. Season with salt and pepper, and more lemon juice to taste.

THE SMILE

Butternut Squash Bread Pudding

Craig Koketsu, QUALITY EATS • *Serves 12 as a side*

Ingredients

2 (1½-pound) loaves brioche or any day-old bread, cut into 1-inch cubes (about 12 cups)

¼ cup (½ stick) unsalted butter

1 (1½ pound) butternut squash, peeled, seeded, and cut into ½-inch chunks (about 2 cups)

1 large or 2 small leeks, white and light green parts only, thinly sliced (about 1 cup)

1 teaspoon fresh thyme leaves

¼ teaspoon cayenne pepper

3 teaspoons Kosher salt, divided

2 teaspoons granulated sugar, divided

3 large eggs

1 large egg yolk

3 cups whole milk

3 cups heavy cream

6 ounces Emmentaler, Comte, and/or Gouda, grated (1 ½ cups), divided

Steps

Preheat oven to 350°F. Line a baking sheet with parchment paper.

Spread the brioche cubes onto the baking sheet and bake, flipping halfway through, until golden brown, 20 to 25 minutes. Remove from the oven, let cool, then transfer to a large mixing bowl.

Heat the butter in a large saucepan over medium heat until melted and foamy. Add the squash and leeks and cook until beginning to soften, about 5 minutes. Add the thyme, cayenne, 1 teaspoon of the salt, and 1 teaspoon of the sugar and stir to combine. Cook until the squash is tender, 5 to 7 minutes. Pour the mixture over the toasted brioche, stir a few times to combine, and set aside.

Whisk the eggs, egg yolk, milk, and cream in a large bowl until combined. Season with the remaining 2 teaspoons salt and 1 teaspoon sugar.

Add 1 cup of the cheese to the bowl with the brioche and veggies and mix until the ingredients are evenly distributed.

Transfer the bread mixture to a 9x13-inch baking dish. Pour two thirds of the custard mixture over the bread and gently press down to saturate all the pieces. Pour the remaining one third of the custard evenly over the bread and let stand for 15 minutes before baking. Top with remaining ½ cup cheese.

Bake until the pudding is set, 55 to 70 minutes. If the top starts to brown too much before the custard sets, place a sheet of tinfoil over top. Remove from the oven and let rest at least 10 minutes before serving.

QUALITY EATS

Mains

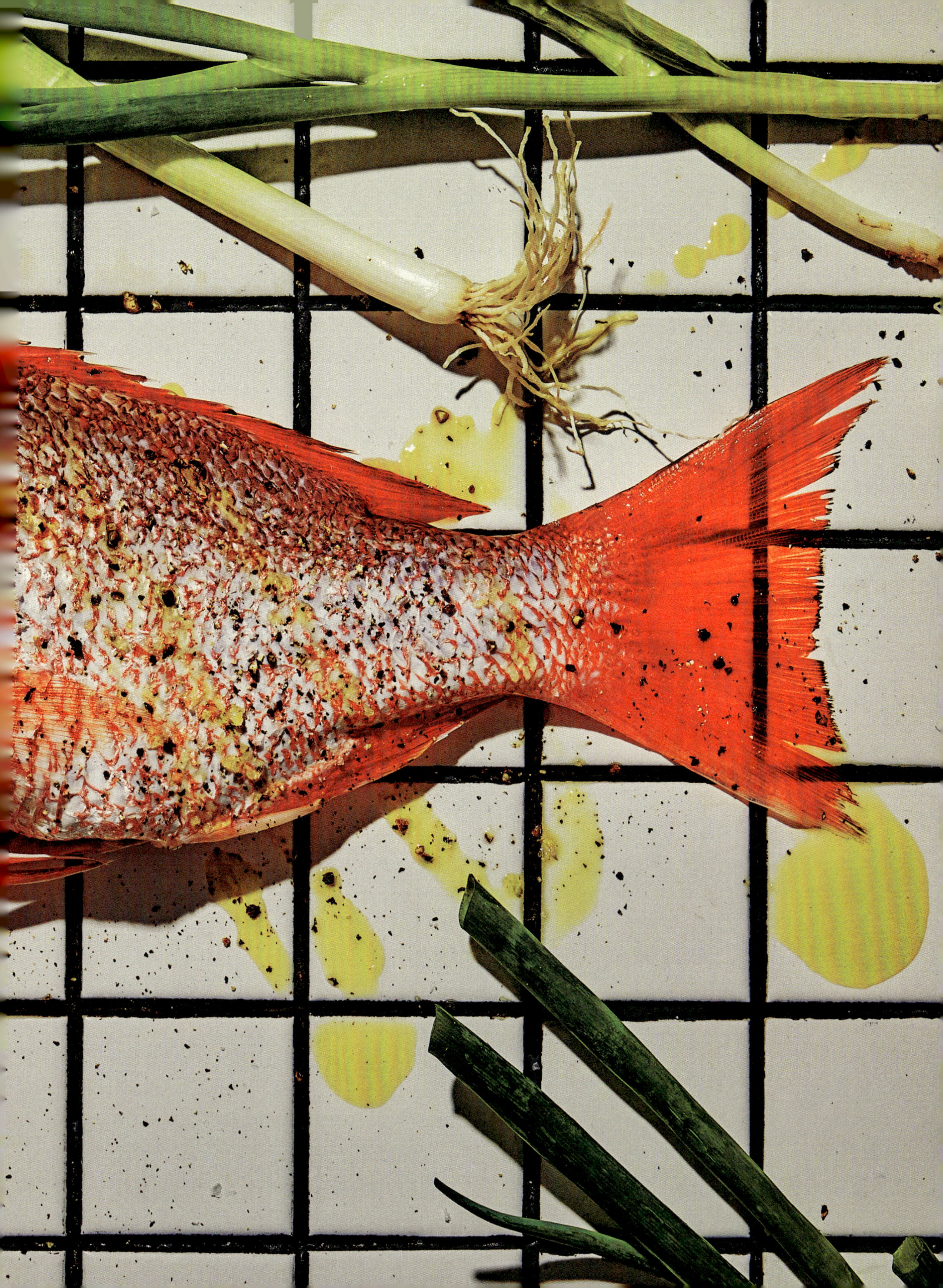

Kimchi Stew with Rice Cakes and Shredded Pork

MOMOFUKU • *Serves 8 to 10*

Ingredients

- 1 3-pound piece of boneless pork shoulder
- 2 tablespoons Kosher salt
- 2 tablespoons sugar
- 3 tablespoons grapeseed or other neutral oil
- 6 onions, thinly sliced
- 8 cups kimchi, preferably a mix of radish and Napa cabbage varieties
- 8 cups chicken or vegetable broth
- 6 tablespoons mirin (or dry white wine, or rice vinegar seasoned with 3 tablespoons sugar)
- 1 cup sliced rice cakes or 1 cup cooked short-grain rice
- 4 scallions, thinly sliced, for serving
- 1 carrot, julienned, for serving

Steps

Put the pork shoulder in a roasting pan or other oven-safe vessel that holds it snugly. Mix salt and sugar in a small bowl and rub all over the meat. Cover vessel with plastic wrap and chill for at least 6 hours, but no longer than 24.

Heat oven to 250°F. Discard any liquid that accumulated in the pan while the meat was in the refrigerator. Roast pork, basting it with the rendered fat and pan juices every hour, until meat is tender enough to be shredded with a fork, about 6 hours. Let pork rest at least 30 minutes before shredding into bite sized pieces.

While pork cooks, prepare the stew. Heat oil in a large pot or Dutch oven over medium-high until shimmering, but not smoking. Add onions—they may almost fill pot—and cook, undisturbed, until bottom layer of onions begins to brown, about 3 minutes. Carefully toss onions, season with salt, and continue to cook, stirring often, until onions have softened and significantly reduced in volume, 15 to 20 minutes. Reduce heat to medium-low and cook, stirring occasionally, until very soft and deep golden brown, 35 to 40 minutes more. Add kimchi and broth, bring to a boil over medium-high heat; reduce heat to medium-low and simmer to allow flavors to meld, 5 to 6 minutes.

Add shredded pork to stew and stir to incorporate and warm through. Add mirin and a few grinds of black pepper. Taste stew and season with additional salt and/or mirin if necessary. (The sweetness of the mirin can tame the sourness of the kimchi, so add more if you feel the need to reel in the kimchi flavor.) Add the rice cakes and cook until warmed through, about 30 seconds. (If you can't find rice cakes, prepare stew and serve with any cooked short-grain rice.) Divide stew among bowls and top with scallions and carrots.

MOMOFUKU

Frittata di Primavera

This delicious frittata is a great way to use up odds and ends in the fridge. At King, we love these flavors of spring, but a fall twist of potatoes, treviso, and prosciutto would also be lovely.

Jess Shadbolt & Clare de Boer, **KING** • *Serves 4*

Ingredients

4 cups water

1 clove garlic, peeled

2 teaspoons Kosher salt, plus more for serving, divided

2 cups frozen peas

1/4 cup extra-virgin olive oil, divided

1 teaspoon freshly ground black pepper, divided

5 large eggs

2 tablespoons crème fraîche or sour cream

1/2 cup (packed) fresh mint leaves, torn

1 small zucchini, shaved into ribbons with a potato peeler

1/4 cup Parmesan, grated, divided

Sea salt, to taste

Steps

Preheat oven to 350°F.

In a small saucepan, combine 4 cups of water, the garlic and 1 teaspoon salt to a boil. Add peas and cook until tender, about 1 to 2 minutes. Drain and discard the garlic. In a small bowl, use a fork to mash half of the peas with 2 tablespoons of olive oil until the mixture is a coarse purée. Season with ½ teaspoon salt and ½ teaspoon pepper. Reserve other half of the peas, keeping them whole. Set aside to cool.

In a large bowl, beat the eggs and crème fraîche and season with ½ teaspoon salt and ½ teaspoon pepper. Add the whole peas, the pea purée, and half of the torn mint leaves.

Heat 1 tablespoon oil in an 8-inch ovenproof skillet over medium high heat. Add egg mixture and top with the zucchini ribbons and remaining mint leaves. Cook until the bottom is set, 3 to 5 minutes.

Top with 2 tablespoons Parmesan, drizzle with remaining tablespoon olive oil and transfer to the oven. Cook until the center of the frittata is just set, 10 to 12 minutes. Remove from oven and top with the remaining Parmesan, and sprinkle with sea salt to finish.

Run a spatula around the frittata to loosen. Let stand 3 minutes to set before serving.

KING

Broccoli and Chickpea Pasta

This is a recipe that my kids have been eating all of their lives and it's a Cookshop fave.

Marc Meyer, **COOKSHOP** • *Serves 4*

Ingredients

1 (15- to 19-ounce) can chickpeas, drained and rinsed

1/2 cup freshly squeezed lemon juice (from 2 lemons)

3/4 cup extra-virgin olive oil, divided

1/2 teaspoon Kosher salt

1/8 teaspoon freshly ground black pepper

1 1/2 pounds broccoli or broccoli rabe, cut into florets (or, if using broccoli rabe, leaves and stems roughly chopped)

1 pound rigatoni or other short pasta

5 cloves garlic, thinly sliced

1 1/2 teaspoons crushed red pepper flakes

1 cup (2 ounces) freshly grated Parmesan cheese, divided

Steps

Add chickpeas, lemon juice, and 1/2 cup of olive oil to a medium bowl and toss to combine. Season with ½ teaspoon salt and ⅛ teaspoon pepper.

Bring a large pot of salted water to a boil. Add broccoli and cook until crisp-tender, about 4 minutes. Using a slotted spoon, transfer broccoli to a colander and rinse under cold water until cool. Return pot of water to a boil, add pasta, and cook to al dente according to package instructions.

Meanwhile, heat the remaining ¼ cup oil in a large high-sided skillet over medium heat. Add garlic and crushed red pepper flake and cook until garlic is golden brown, about 4 minutes. Add broccoli and cook until tender, about 5 minutes. Add chickpea mixture and cook until warm, 1 minute more.

Drain pasta, reserving ¼ cup of cooking water. Add pasta and reserved water to broccoli and chickpeas and season with salt and pepper, to taste. Cook, stirring, until pasta is coated with sauce. Add ½ cup Parmesan and toss to combine. Transfer to a large bowl, sprinkle with remaining ½ cup Parmesan, and serve.

COOKSHOP

Korean-Style Rice and Eggs

Not sure if this is worthy of being called a "recipe," but it's something that's really nostalgic for me as a Korean-American. It's what I made for myself as a kid when there was nothing at home and my mom was out. It's basically a delicious comfort-struggle meal—super simple, requires minimal ingredients, and impossible to mess up. We always make big batches of rice, portion it out, and freeze it for easy access. And for those asking if they can just add the sesame oil and soy sauce to the rice at the same time, the answer is no. The order matters—trust.

Sam Yoo, GOLDEN DINER • *Serves 1*

Ingredients

- 1 cup cooked short- or medium-grain white rice (leftover is fine)
- 2 eggs
- 2 teaspoons sesame oil
- 2 teaspoons soy sauce
- Grated cheese, butter, sesame seeds, and/or kimchi, for serving, optional

Steps

If using cold or leftover rice, heat up rice in whatever manner you please.

Meanwhile, prepare eggs in whatever style you like best. (I like mine sunny side up with an extra gooey yolk, so it oozes out and coats the rice.)

When the rice is hot, transfer it to a bowl and gently mix in sesame oil. Add a bit of grated cheese and butter, if using. Lay the eggs on top of the rice and spoon the soy sauce overtop. Top with sesame seeds and/or kimchi if you're feeling extra fancy.

GOLDEN DINER

Khichdi

Khichdi is an age-old, Ayurvedic comfort dish that has had a recent rise in popularity due to its many wellness properties. Traditionally, it is cooked to help treat all kinds of imbalances, particularly when people have a weakened immune system. It can be eaten for breakfast, lunch, or dinner. It is nourishing, grounding, warming, cleansing, and easy to digest. It's a perfect dish during these times of high stress and anxiety.

Sydne Gooden, INDAY • *Serves 3 to 4*

Ingredients

- 1 cup whole mung beans, soaked overnight
- ½ cup brown basmati rice, soaked overnight
- ½ yellow onion, minced
- 4 tablespoons coconut oil, divided
- 1½-inch piece fresh ginger, peeled and finely chopped
- 2 cloves garlic, minced
- 1 red fresno chile, minced, optional
- 2 teaspoons cumin seed
- 1 ½ teaspoons fennel seed
- 1 ¼ teaspoon mustard seed
- 2 teaspoons ground coriander
- ½ teaspoon ground turmeric
- 1 large sweet potato, peeled and cut into 1-inch cubes
- Kosher salt or sea salt
- 1 bay leaf
- 5 cups vegetable broth
- Chopped fresh cilantro, lime wedges, and vegan or regular yogurt, for serving

Steps

Heat 2 tablespoons coconut oil in a large pot over medium heat. Add onion and cook, stirring often, until beginning to brown, 5 to 7 minutes. Add ginger, garlic, and chile, if using. Cook, stirring, 1 to 2 minutes.

Push ingredients to the sides of the pot to make a well in the center. Add remaining 2 tablespoons coconut oil, cumin, fennel, and mustard seeds and cook, stirring constantly, until lightly toasted, about 1 minute. Add mung beans, coriander, and turmeric and stir to combine. Cook, stirring occasionally, 3 to 4 minutes.

Add rice and sweet potato and season with ¼ teaspoon salt. Cook, stirring often and scraping the bottom of the pot, about 3 minutes. Add bay leaf and 2 cups broth and bring to a simmer. Add remaining broth, 1 cup at a time, stirring, and waiting for the simmer before adding the next batch of broth, about 6 minutes total. Keep incorporating stock until rice and mung beans are tender and mixture takes on a porridge-like texture, stirring occasionally, 25 to 30 minutes.

Season to taste with ½ teaspoon salt and serve with lime wedges, cilantro, and yogurt.

INDAY

Butter Beans, 'Nduja, Leeks and Lemon

This dish was developed from things I had in my pantry. I find that a salad of soft, warm beans is very comforting. Plus, there is the satisfaction I get from cooking beans perfectly soft, without them exploding.

Jaime Young, SUNDAY IN BROOKLYN • *Serves 4*

Ingredients

1 cup dried butter beans

1/3 cup olive oil, plus one teaspoon, divided

6 ounces 'nduja sausage or spicy Italian sausage, casings removed

1 teaspoon fresh thyme leaves

1/8 teaspoon chili flakes

2 bay leaves

6 garlic cloves, peeled

1 sprig rosemary

2 teaspoons Kosher salt, plus more to taste

1 tablespoon unsalted butter

2 medium leeks, white and light green parts only, thinly sliced into 1/4-inch rounds

Freshly ground black pepper, to taste

1 tablespoon lemon juice

1 teaspoon lemon zest

1/4 cup fresh parsley, freshly chopped

Steps

Place the beans in a large saucepan and cover with two inches of water. Set aside to soak overnight.

The next day, drain the beans and place them in a large saucepan with the olive oil, thyme, chili flakes, bay leaves, garlic, and rosemary. Cover with 3 cups of water and bring to a boil over high heat. Reduce the heat to maintain a gentle simmer and cook until the beans are tender, 45 minutes. Remove the beans from the heat, add the salt, and set aside to cool in their cooking liquid.

Meanwhile. In a large skillet, In a separate medium sauté pan, heat 1 teaspoon olive oil over medium heat. Crumble in the 'nduja and cook, using a spatula to break it into smaller pieces, about 3 minutes. Pour off oil to reserve for later and set 'nduja aside to cool.

In a large skillet melt the butter over medium heat. Add the leeks and season with a generous pinch of salt and pepper. Cook, stirring occasionally, until almost soft, 4 minutes. Add beans (and their cooking liquid), and continue cooking until the liquid becomes saucy and reduces, 3 to 5 minutes. Turn off heat, stir in lemon juice and zest. Set aside and keep warm.

To assemble, add warm beans and leeks to a small bowl. Top with the 'nduja and drizzle with the reserved cooking oil. Sprinkle with the parsley and black pepper to serve.

SUNDAY IN BROOKLYN

Pasta with White Wine Sauce and Spring Vegetables

The NoMad serves this dish with homemade cavatelli in a buttery broth with lots of spring vegetables and a poached egg on top. If you don't want to make cavatelli, substitute whatever short pasta you prefer. As for the spring vegetables, we've used asparagus and peas, but this dish would be delicious with almost anything you have in your fridge. Crispy shaved radishes and fava bean leaves are beautiful for garnish and add a crunchy texture to finish the dish.

THE NOMAD • *Serves 4*

Ingredients

White Wine Sauce
- 1 cup white wine
- 1 celery stalk, thinly sliced
- 1 small onion, thinly sliced
- 1 small carrot, thinly sliced
- 2 whole button mushrooms, thinly sliced
- 4 cups chicken stock or broth
- 1 bay leaf
- 11 tablespoons butter, cut into ½-inch pieces
- Kosher salt, to taste

Pasta and Assembly
- 1 pound cavatelli or other short pasta
- 1 bunch asparagus, trimmed and cut into 1-inch pieces
- 1⅓ cups frozen peas, thawed
- 1½ cups snap peas, halved on the bias
- 1 bunch small radishes, divided
- 4 tablespoons unsalted butter

Steps

Combine wine, celery, onion, carrot, and mushrooms in a medium pot. Bring to a boil over high heat, then reduce heat and simmer until the pan is almost dry, 10 to 12 minutes. Add the chicken stock and bay leaf to the saucepan and continue to simmer, 20 minutes. Strain the sauce (about 2 cups) into a clean saucepan. Gradually add the butter, a couple pieces at a time, whisking after each addition until melted and emulsified. Season with salt. Turn off heat.

Bring a large pot of salted water to a boil. Add pasta and cook according to package directions for al dente.

Meanwhile, bring ¾ cup of the white wine sauce to a simmer in a large skillet. Add asparagus, peas, snap peas, and 8 radishes cut into quarters. Cover and cook, 2 minutes. When pasta is al dente, transfer to the skillet using a slotted spoon. Add butter and continue to cook, stirring gently, until sauce reduces and coats the pasta and vegetables, 3 to 4 minutes. Divide among shallow bowls. Using a mandolin or sharp knife, thinly slice remaining radishes and scatter over top of each bowl.

Freeze any remaining white wine sauce for later use.

THE NOMAD

Roasted Market Fish with Ginger Scallion Sauce

I love making this dish for a crowd because it's so easy, delicious, and versatile. Use almost any 1 to 2 pound fish, season well, and slather in your favorite ginger scallion sauce. Leave it at that for a few people at home, or garnish with herbs, citrus, fried shallots, and pickled red chilis to step it up a bit. This dish can be anything you want it to be, with no fuss either way.

Julie Cole, **NOM WAH NOLITA** • *Serves 4*

Ingredients

Ginger Scallion Sauce

- 3 whole scallions, finely chopped
- 2 tablespoons finely chopped fresh ginger (from 1-inch piece)
- 1/2 cup plus 2 tablespoons canola or other neutral oil
- 1/4 teaspoon light soy sauce
- 1/4 teaspoon rice vinegar
- 1/4 teaspoon Kosher salt

Fish and Assembly

- 2 small whole fish (1 to 2 pounds each), such as branzino, black bass, red bass, gutted and scaled
- 2 tablespoons canola or other neutral oil, plus more for baking sheet
- Kosher salt, to season
- Freshly ground black, to season
- 1 lemon, thinly sliced, plus 1 lemon, halved
- 2 whole scallions, trimmed and thinly sliced
- Fresh cilantro, for serving

Steps

Make the Ginger Scallion Sauce: Combine chopped scallions and ginger in a small heatproof bowl. In a small saucepan, heat oil over medium-high heat until hot. Carefully pour oil over scallions and ginger. Stir with a spoon to combine. Add soy sauce, vinegar, and salt. Stir to combine. Let cool to room temperature.

Make the fish: Preheat oven to 425°F. Pat the fish dry, inside and out. Brush with 1 tablespoon oil and season all over, including inside the cavity, with salt and pepper. Tuck lemon slices and some scallions inside the fish.

Line a baking sheet with foil and lightly brush with oil. Place fish on foil. Roast, until a fork pierces through the flesh with no resistance and fish is opaque and cooked through, 18 to 22 minutes, depending on size.

Meanwhile, heat remaining 1 tablespoon oil in a small cast iron pan or skillet over high heat. When the oil is almost smoking, add the lemon halves, cut side down. Cook, undisturbed, until charred, 2 minutes. Transfer to a plate.

Transfer fish to a large plate or platter. Remove and discard lemon slices from the cavity.

Stir the ginger scallion sauce and pour over fish. Top with remaining scallions and cilantro and serve with charred lemons and any remaining ginger scallion sauce.

NOM WAH NOLITA

Sweet and Sour Brisket

This may be a restaurant dish, but we love it because it really feels like sitting down to family dinner. It's a great way to use up some of those odds and ends that have been kicking around in your kitchen. Don't have a brisket but do have a chuck roast in the freezer? No problem! (Just keep an eye on the cook time.) We serve our brisket with egg noodles, but any rice, pasta, or potato will work well.

Mike Cain, GERTIE • *Serves 8*

Ingredients

1 4-pound piece point- or flat-cut brisket

Kosher salt

Freshly ground black pepper

3 tablespoons extra-virgin olive oil

3 medium onions, sliced

3 garlic cloves, roughly chopped

1 teaspoon coriander seed

½ teaspoon ground allspice

1 cup whole-berry or smooth canned cranberry sauce

1 cup tomato sauce

4 cups beef stock

1 cup cider vinegar, divided

6 tablespoons butter

6 tablespoons flour

Steps

Preheat oven to 325°F. Season brisket liberally with kosher salt and black pepper. Heat a large Dutch oven or heavy-bottomed pot over medium heat. Sear brisket on all four sides until deeply browned, about 15 to 20 minutes total; transfer brisket to a platter. Reduce heat to medium-low and add olive oil and onions. Cook onions, stirring occasionally, until golden brown and beginning to caramelize, about 15 to 20 minutes. Add the garlic, coriander, and allspice and stir to combine; cook, stirring, until spices are fragrant, about 1 minute. Add cranberry and tomato sauce and season with salt and pepper. Cook, stirring occasionally, until mixture comes to a simmer, about 5 minutes, then add stock and ½ cup vinegar and allow to come to a simmer again. Return brisket to pot; you want the liquid to come about ¾ of the way up the brisket. Bring to a simmer, cover with tight-fitting lid or foil, and slide into the oven. Braise until meat is fork tender, about 4 hours. (Start checking after 3 hours; resist the urge to check on it too early or too often.)

Transfer brisket to a cutting board. With a large soup spoon, try to skim as much fat as possible from the top of the braising liquid. Strain liquid through a fine mesh sieve; reserve liquid and discard solids. Wipe out pot and return to stove; heat over medium. Add butter and, once it melts and foams, slowly whisk in flour a bit at a time. Cook, whisking often, until flour begins to smell a bit nutty but does not take on any color, about 4 minutes. Slowly whisk in 3 cups of reserved braising liquid until fully combined. Bring gravy to a simmer and cook, stirring occasionally, until flavors meld, about 5 minutes. Whisk in remaining ½ cup vinegar and remove from heat. Slice brisket, transfer to platter, and serve with gravy alongside.

GERTIE

Spaghetto al Pomodoro

If there's one dish – just one dish – that represents Italy, it's lo spaghetto al pomodoro. With just five simple ingredients, the Eataly chefs in Italy spent months testing, tasting, and experimenting with different ingredients from the Eataly marketplace in order to create the perfect recipe. Taste it for yourself at either Eataly New York location, or find the ingredients at Eataly to make this iconic plate at home. Buon appetito!

Enrico Panero, **EATALY NEW YORK** • *Serves 4*

Ingredients

1 pound spaghetti

Kosher salt

1 28-ounce can whole peeled tomatoes

¼ cup extra-virgin olive oil, plus more for serving

1½ teaspoons sea salt

3 to 4 sprigs fresh basil

Steps

Cook spaghetti in a large pot of well-salted boiling water until al dente.
   Meanwhile, crush tomatoes between your fingers, letting them fall into a wide heavy pot. Stir in tomato juices, olive oil, and sea salt.
   Reserving ½ cup pasta cooking liquid, drain pasta and transfer to saucepan with tomato mixture. Add pasta cooking liquid. Cook over medium heat, stirring until pasta is coated with sauce, about 1 minute. Adjust seasoning to taste.
   Divide spaghetti into four warmed bowls. Drizzle with olive oil and top with basil. Serve immediately.

EATALY NEW YORK

Signature Burger

Our burger has been our most popular dish since its debut and we love it just as much as our guests do. We use a blend of 80-20 beef, but you can use whatever you like—including a blend of meats if you prefer. We don't use any special marinade or seasoning to maximize flavor of our burger, but we do season it on all sides (not just top and bottom!) with a lot of salt and pepper. That helps gives it a really nice crust.

Reed Adelson, VIRGINIA'S • *Serves 4*

Ingredients

3 tablespoons olive oil

2 medium yellow onions, thinly sliced

Kosher salt and freshly ground black pepper, to taste

1 tablespoon red wine

1½ pounds ground beef

2 tablespoons grapeseed oil or canola oil

4 brioche buns, toasted if desired

Mayonnaise, to serve

Steps

Heat olive oil in a medium skillet over medium-high heat. Add onions and season with salt. Cook, stirring occasionally, until soft and golden, 8 to 10 minutes. Deglaze with the wine, scraping the bottom of the skillet, and cover to keep warm.

Form beef into four equal-sized patties, about 4x4-inches wide and 1-inch thick. Season aggressively all over (remember the sides!) with salt and pepper. Heat a large cast-iron skillet over high. Once the pan is very hot, add oil and burgers and cook, flipping just once, until cooked to desired doneness, about 3 minutes on each side for medium-rare. Transfer the burgers to a cutting board to rest for 5 minutes.

Serve with toasted buns (if desired), mayonnaise, caramelized onions, and additional condiments of your choice.

VIRGINIA'S

White Bean and Spinach Stew

A humble ode to José Andrés, who is always on the front line of the food crisis.

This is a semi-loose take off a Moorish stew made with chickpeas and saffron. I had it in D.C. at José Andrés' Jaleo. I use white beans here and skip the saffron—what I like about this recipe is that it is highly malleable. As far as the pea/bean component, use what you have in your cupboard (like kidney beans or cranberry beans) or cook off those dried beans (scarlet runner beans, anyone?). The recipe is vegan, but you can add beef or chicken stock in place of the water/vegetable stock. You can simmer in some diced chicken or add in sautéed ground beef or turkey. It will fill you up without breaking the bank.

Matt Griffin, SIMON & THE WHALE • *Serves 3 to 4*

Ingredients

- ½ cup plus 1 teaspoon extra-virgin olive oil, divided, plus more for serving
- 1½ cups day-old bread, torn into crouton-sized pieces
- Kosher salt
- ¼ cup finely chopped garlic (about 6 large cloves), divided
- 1 tablespoon chopped flat-leaf parsley, plus more for serving
- 1 tablespoon smoked paprika
- 1 teaspoon ground cumin
- ½ teaspoon cayenne pepper
- 1 15-ounce can cannellini or butter beans, rinsed and drained
- 1½ cups water or vegetable stock
- 3 tablespoons sherry vinegar
- Freshly ground black pepper
- 3 cups baby spinach
- ½ lemon, for serving

Steps

Line a large plate with a layer of paper towels. Set aside.

Heat ¼ cup oil in a large skillet over medium-high heat until hot but not smoking. Add bread and toss to coat. Season with pinch salt and, if bread appears dry, drizzle with oil to coat. Cook, shaking pan frequently, until bread begins to crisp, about 3 minutes.

Add 1 teaspoon oil and 2 tablespoons garlic to skillet with bread. Cook, stirring frequently, until garlic is lightly golden and bread is crisp, 2 to 3 minutes. Add parsley, season with good pinch salt, and toss to combine. Remove skillet from heat and drain croutons on prepared paper towel-lined plate. (These croutons are great on their own. If you want to skip the rest of the recipe and make a salad instead, now's your chance.)

Heat remaining ¼ cup oil and 2 tablespoons garlic in a medium saucepan over medium heat. Cook until fragrant, about 1 minute, then add paprika, cumin, and cayenne. Let spices sizzle a few seconds, then add beans, water or stock, vinegar, pinch salt, and a few grinds black pepper.

Bring to a simmer, then add croutons and return to a simmer. Add spinach and cook until wilted, about 5 minutes. Remove from heat and season to taste with salt. Transfer to your favorite bowl, finish with a drizzle of olive oil, squeeze of lemon, and fresh parsley. Serve warm.

SIMON & THE WHALE

Pasta e Fagioli

To us, pasta fagioli is the ultimate Italian-American soul food that comes together fairly quickly for a hearty and comforting meal.

Angie Rito & Scott Tacinelli, **DON ANGIE** • *Serves 6 to 8*

Ingredients

½ cup pancetta or bacon, finely chopped

1 cup extra-virgin olive oil, divided

7 garlic cloves, finely chopped

1 teaspoon crushed red pepper flakes

1½ tablespoons Kosher salt

1½ teaspoons freshly ground black pepper, plus more for serving

1 bunch scallions, white and pale green parts thinly sliced, dark green parts reserved for serving

1 bunch chopped greens, such as collards or kale, fresh or frozen (tough ribs removed, if fresh)

1 large lemon, zested and juiced

1 15-oz can beans, such as black-eyed peas or chickpeas, drained and rinsed (If using dried beans, cook according to package instructions)

8 cups low-sodium chicken stock

1½ cups (10 oz) uncooked short pasta, such as ditalini, or long pasta such as linguine, broken into 1-inch pieces

Pinch of sugar

1 cup (4 oz) grated Parmesan, divided

Steps

Combine pancetta or bacon and ½ cup oil in a large pot over medium heat. Cook, stirring occasionally, until the fat has rendered from meat, about 3 minutes. Add garlic, crushed red pepper, salt, and pepper and stir to combine. Cook, stirring constantly, until the garlic is fragrant and lightly toasted, about 1 minute. Add the scallion whites and pale green parts, and cook, stirring often, until translucent, 2 to 3 minutes.

Add greens, lemon zest, and lemon juice, and cook, stirring often, until greens are completely wilted and softened, about 5 minutes for frozen greens and up to 12 minutes for heartier, fresh greens. Add beans and stock and bring to a boil over medium-high heat, reduce heat to medium-low and simmer for 10 minutes. Add pasta and cook until pasta is just tender, about 8 minutes. Stir in sugar and ½ cup cheese. Spoon into serving bowls and top with remaining ½ cup cheese and ½ cup olive oil. Finish with freshly cracked black pepper and scallion greens.

DON ANGIE

Mac and Cheese

At Dig Inn, we consider mac & cheese a vegetable. Our signature mac uses a custom blend of cheeses from Jasper Hill Farm in Vermont, but use whatever kind of hard cheeses make you happy. There are a few steps to this recipe, but unlike just opening up a box, this homemade recipe will give you mad bragging rights. Bake it and share it, or keep all the deliciousness for yourself...we won't judge.

Matt Weingarten, DIG INN • *Serves 8*

Ingredients

Seasoned Bread Crumbs

- 1 cup panko bread crumbs
- 2 teaspoons smoked paprika
- 1/2 teaspoon fresh rosemary, minced
- 1 teaspoon fine sea salt
- 1/4 teaspoon freshly ground black pepper
- 1 tablespoon olive oil

Mac & Cheese

- Unsalted butter, for the pan
- 1 (16-ounce) package elbow macaroni
- 1/3 cup olive oil
- 1/3 cup whole wheat flour
- 1 tablespoon fine sea salt, plus more for the pasta water and to taste
- 1/2 teaspoon nutmeg
- 1/4 teaspoon freshly ground black pepper, plus more to taste
- 2 quarts (8 cups) whole milk
- 1 sprig rosemary
- 20 ounces (5 cups) mixed hard cheese, shredded (we use a blend from Jasper Hill, but any good Cheddar, Gruyere, or Fontina cheese works well)

Steps

Make the seasoned bread crumbs: In a medium bowl, mix the panko, paprika, rosemary, salt, pepper and olive oil and to combine.

Heat the oven to 400°F. Grease a 9-inch-by-13-inch baking dish with butter.

Make the mac & cheese: In a large pot over high heat, bring generously salted water to a boil. Add the pasta and stir immediately to ensure the noodles don't stick together. Cook until just al dente, according to package instructions. Drain and set aside.

Meanwhile, in a large saucepan over medium-low heat, heat the oil. Use a wooden spoon to stir in the flour, salt, nutmeg, and pepper. Cook, stirring constantly, for 3 minutes, taking care not to color the flour. Slowly add the milk and, use a whisk to vigorously stir, breaking up any lumps, until combined. Add the rosemary sprig and increase the heat to medium-high. Bring to a boil and lower heat, stirring occasionally to make sure the mixture does not scorch. Cook until thickened slightly, about 5 minutes, or until it has the consistency of heavy cream. Remove from the heat and pass through a fine-mesh strainer into a saucepan. Keep warm over low heat. Makes 7 ½ cups.

Stir cheese into the sauce until melted and season with salt and pepper.

Add pasta to the cheese sauce. Stir to coat, then transfer the mixture to the prepared baking dish. Sprinkle evenly with the bread crumbs and cover with aluminum foil. Place the baking dish on a foil-lined baking sheet to catch any drips.

Bake for 10 minutes. Remove the foil and bake for another 8 to 10 minutes, until the breadcrumbs are toasted and the sauce is bubbling. Allow to cool for at least 10 minutes before serving.

DIG INN

Galbi Bowl

Galbi is one of the most comforting dishes to me. The beef is both sweet and savory thanks to the marinade, which marries soy sauce with brown sugar, ripe pears, and tart orange juice. When paired with homemade pickled daikon—both refreshing and spicy at the same time—I am immediately transported to my happy place. Take care to move the meat around the pan and deglaze as you cook; the marinade is packed with sugar, so it may burn if not closely watched. When cooked correctly, the meat develops a nice, even glaze.

Simon Kim, **COTE** • *Serves 4 to 6*

Ingredients

Short Ribs

- 1¼ cups soy sauce
- 1½ cups water
- 1 cup packed brown sugar
- ½ cup plus 1 tablespoon mirin
- 3 pears, cored and chopped
- ⅔ cup orange juice
- 1 medium onion, chopped
- ½ cup garlic cloves, peeled
- 1 (1-inch) piece fresh ginger, peeled
- 5 pounds (½-inch-thick) flanken-style beef short ribs

Pickled Daikon and Assembly

- 3 large or 4 small daikon radishes, turnips, or carrots, cut into ¼-inch cubes
- 1½ cups sugar
- 1¼ cups rice wine vinegar
- ¼ cup water
- 1½ teaspoons salt
- 1 tablespoon vegetable oil
- Steamed rice, for serving

Steps

For short ribs: Combine soy sauce, water, sugar, mirin, pears, orange juice, onion, garlic, and ginger in a blender and purée until smooth. Strain through a fine-mesh sieve and transfer to large glass (or plastic) container or baking dish. Add short ribs and toss to coat. Marinate, refrigerated, at least 4 hours, or overnight.

For pickles: Meanwhile, place radishes, turnips, or carrots in a medium heatproof container. Combine sugar, rice wine vinegar, water, and salt in a small saucepan and bring to a boil, then remove from heat and pour over daikon. Let cool to room temperature, then refrigerate until ready to use.

Remove ribs from fridge 30 minutes before cooking. When ready to cook, remove short ribs from marinade, letting excess drip off. Discard remaining marinade. Heat oil in a large skillet over medium-high heat. Cook short ribs in batches, undisturbed, until golden on underside, 3 to 4 minutes, then flip. Continue cooking, turning occasionally, until meat is glazed and edges begin to char, about 4 minutes more.

Serve short ribs over rice and top with pickled veg.

COTE

Al's French Toast Anglaise

During brunch service, Crown Shy feels more like a neighborhood restaurant than usual, as people who live in the building mosey down with their kids for the first meal of the day. Now that everyone is at home, this french toast method works at any time of day, any day of the week. We typically serve it with a homemade meyer lemon marmalade, but use any jam you have sitting in the fridge.

James Kent, CROWN SHY • *Serves 10*

Ingredients

- 2 cups heavy cream
- 6 large egg yolks
- 1/2 cups sugar
- 1/2 teaspoon Kosher salt
- 1/2 vanilla bean, split lengthwise or 1 teaspoon vanilla extract
- 4 strips orange zest, removed with a vegetable peeler
- 1 loaf brioche or challah, sliced into 10, 3/4-inch slices
- Vegetable oil, for frying
- Unsalted butter, for frying

Steps

Preheat oven to 400°F. In a medium saucepan, combine heavy cream, egg yolks, sugar, and salt over medium heat. Cook, whisking constantly, until sugar is dissolved and mixture is slightly thickened, about 8 minutes. Remove from heat, add the vanilla bean and orange zest. Let steep for 20 minutes. Remove bean and zest; discard. Custard can be made up to 3 days ahead.

Place custard in a shallow 9x13-inch baking dish. Arrange the bread on a wire rack set in a rimmed baking sheet and allow to dry for 10 to 15 minutes. Working one piece at a time, submerge bread slices in the custard and turn to coat. Return slices to the rack and let drain.

Working in batches, heat about 1 teaspoon each oil and butter in a nonstick pan over medium high heat. When the oil-butter mixture is foaming, add coated bread and cook, flipping halfway through, until golden brown on both sides, about 2½ minutes per side. Transfer to a clean spot on the wire rack, or another wire rack set in a rimmed baking sheet. Wipe out pan and repeat process with remaining batches. Transfer toast to the oven and cook until crisp, about 10 minutes. Let cool before serving.

CROWN SHY

Pastrami Potato Hash

A few basic ingredients to hit the spot! The seasoning of the pastrami flavors the whole dish, so there is no need for extra salt and pepper or spices. Recipe from *Remington Camp Cooking* by Charlie Palmer.

Charlie Palmer, CHARLIE PALMER STEAK • *Serves 4 to 6*

Ingredients

1/4 cup vegetable oil

1 pound Yukon Gold potatoes (about 3 potatoes), cut into 1/2-inch pieces

1/4 teaspoon sea salt

1/2 large white onion, cut into 1/4-inch pieces (about 1 cup)

1 red bell pepper, cored, seeded, and cut into 1/4-inch pieces (about 1 cup)

3/4 pound pastrami, cut into 1/4-inch pieces (about 3 cups)

4 to 6 large eggs, fried, scrambled, or cooked to your liking

2 scallions, thinly sliced into rounds, for serving

Steps

Heat oil in a 12-inch cast-iron skillet over high heat until shimmering. Add potatoes and cook, undisturbed, until golden brown, 5 to 7 minutes. Toss once and leave undisturbed until mostly golden, 2 minutes more. Add salt.

Add onion and bell pepper, and cook, stirring occasionally, until just tender, 2 to 3 minutes. Stir in pastrami and cook until meat is browned in spots and potatoes are fork tender, about 5 minutes.

Serve topped with eggs and scallions.

CHARLIE PALMER STEAK

Cajun Rib Steak

Elman Gallardo, SMITH & WOLLENSKY • *Serves 4*

Ingredients

- 1 tablespoon cayenne pepper
- 1 tablespoon chili powder
- 1 tablespoon garlic powder
- 1 tablespoon ground black pepper
- 1 tablespoon ground white pepper
- 1 tablespoon onion powder
- 1 tablespoon smoked paprika
- 1½ teaspoons ground cumin
- 1 teaspoon dried basil
- 1 teaspoon dried oregano
- 1 teaspoon dried thyme
- 1 USDA prime rib steak or skirt steak (1½ to 2 pounds)
- 2 to 3 cups vegetable oil, depending on size and cut of meat, plus 2 tablespoons for cooking
- 2 white onions, finely chopped
- ½ cup apple cider vinegar
- 2 tablespoons Kosher salt, plus more for steak
- 2 tablespoons brown sugar (light or dark)

Steps

In a medium bowl, whisk together cayenne, chili powder, garlic powder, black and white pepper, onion powder, paprika, cumin, basil, oregano, and thyme.

In a large skillet, add Cajun spice mix and toast over medium heat, stirring continuously, until fragrant, 3 to 5 minutes. Remove from heat and immediately transfer to a small bowl to cool. Once cooled, rub meat generously on all sides with 6½ tablespoons Cajun spice mix. Transfer steak to a plate and refrigerate, uncovered, for 1 hour.

In a large bowl, combine 2 cups oil, onion, vinegar, 2 tablespoons salt, sugar, and remaining 2 tablespoons Cajun spice mix. Remove steak from refrigerator, add to bowl, and turn to coat. If using skirt steak, cut in 3 pieces so it fits in skillet when cooking. If marinade doesn't fully cover the meat, stir in up to an additional cup of oil until meat is just submerged. Cover, refrigerate, and marinate overnight (or up to 48 hours).

Preheat oven to 350°F. Remove steak from marinade and wipe off any excess marinade. Season all over with salt. Heat remaining 2 tablespoons oil in a large cast-iron skillet over high heat. Add the steak and cook, flipping once, until charred on each side, 6 to 8 minutes total. If using skirt steak, cook in batches, if needed. Transfer to a sheet tray and finish in the oven for 8 to 10 minutes for medium-rare.

Transfer the steak to a baking sheet fitted with a wire rack and let rest for 10 minutes. Transfer to a cutting board to slice and serve.

SMITH & WOLLENSKY

Indonesian Chicken with Vermicelli Noodles

I love making this dish as it reminds my family and me of the incredible street food we eat in Jakarta, Indonesia—my wife Ochi's hometown. During the quarantine, Ochi requested I make this dish in particular as she's been missing and craving her favorite Indonesian foods now more than ever.

Cedric Vongerichten, WAYAN • *Serves 4*

Ingredients

4 large eggs

1/4 pound vermicelli rice noodles or any type of pasta

8 skin-on, bone-in chicken thighs
Kosher salt

2 tablespoons olive oil

2 tablespoons unsalted butter

1 medium yellow onion, sliced

5 garlic cloves, coarsely chopped

1/2 cup dry white wine

3 cups chicken stock, vegetable stock, or water

2 tablespoons curry powder, optional

1/2 cup coconut milk

1/4 cup roughly chopped cilantro

4 scallions, sliced

1 lime, cut into 4 wedges

Steps

Bring a medium saucepan of water to a boil. Gently add eggs and reduce heat to a rapid simmer. Cook for 6 minutes. Remove pan from heat. Using a slotted spoon, transfer eggs to a bowl of ice water. Let cool at least 5 minutes.

Meanwhile, cook noodles in lightly salted water according to package directions, then drain. Set aside. Drain, then peel eggs. Set aside.

Pat chicken dry and season generously with salt. In a very large skillet, heat oil and butter over medium-high heat. Add chicken, skin side-down and in a single layer (cook in batches, if necessary to avoid crowding skillet). Cook undisturbed, until skin is golden-brown and crisp, 5 to 8 minutes. Transfer to a plate.

Reduce heat to medium. Add onion and garlic to skillet. Cook, stirring occasionally, until translucent, about 5 minutes. Add wine and cook until liquid reduces by half, 1 to 2 minutes more. Add chicken stock and curry powder, if using, then arrange chicken pieces on top of onion mixture, skin side-up.

Bring liquid just to a boil over high heat, then reduce heat to maintain a simmer. Cook until thermometer inserted into thickest part of chicken reads 165°F, 10 to 15 minutes, depending on size. (Remove pieces as finished, then return to pan once all chicken is cooked through.) Stir in the coconut milk and simmer 5 minutes more. Remove from heat.

Divide reserved noodles among four bowls. Top with chicken and sauce. With your hands, halve a reserved egg over each bowl. Top with cilantro and scallions, and serve with lime wedges.

WAYAN

Sweets

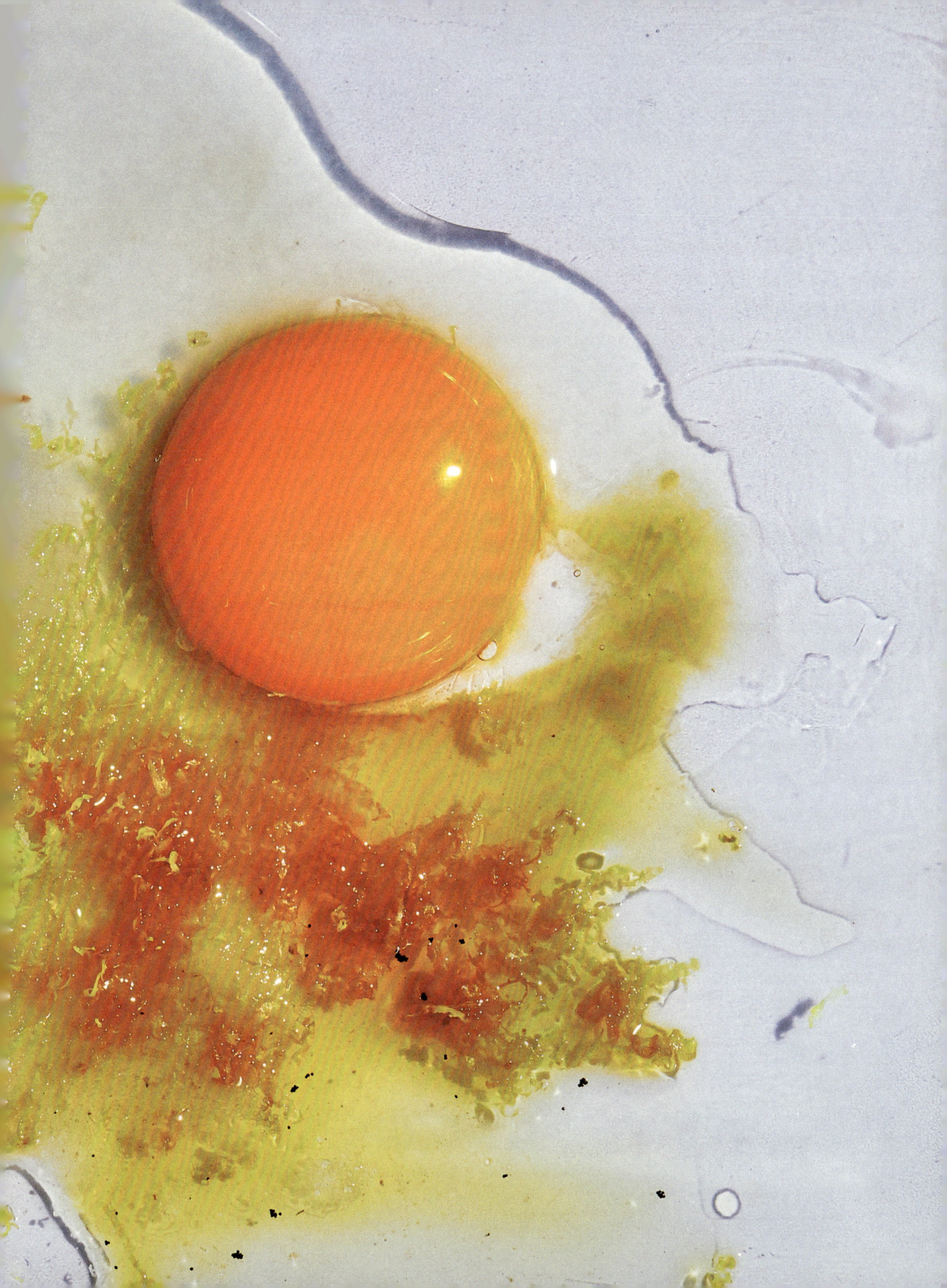

Olive Oil Cake

Our olive oil cake is one of the few dishes on the Hart's menu that never leaves. We love it not only for its simplicity, but also because it is a great accompaniment to the present season's fruits, whatever that season may be. In the summer, we serve it with lightly roasted blueberries or raspberries with a splash of lemon juice, olive oil, and a pinch of sugar. In the winter, we serve it with poached quince or even just some toasted hazelnuts and honey. This cake is both comforting and inspiring!

Katie Jackson and Nick Perkins, **HART'S** • *Serves 6 to 8*

Ingredients

- 3/4 cup extra-virgin olive oil, plus more for the pan
- 3/4 cup all-purpose flour, sifted, plus more for the pan
- 1 cup sugar, divided
- 3 tablespoons lemon juice
- 1 teaspoon lemon zest
- 2 large egg yolks
- 1 teaspoon vanilla extract
- 3 large egg whites
- 1 teaspoon Kosher salt
- Whipped cream, for serving
- Berries, for serving
- Toasted nuts, honey, or jam, for serving

Steps

Preheat oven to 350°F. Lightly coat a 9-inch round cake pan with olive oil and line the bottom with parchment paper. Oil the parchment and flour the pan, tapping out any excess flour.

In an electric mixer fitted with a whisk attachment, beat ½ cup sugar with the lemon juice and zest, egg yolks, and vanilla extract on medium speed until incorporated. Add flour, in 4 additions, making sure it is incorporated between each addition. With the mixer running, gradually drizzle in the olive oil. Use a rubber spatula to scrape down the sides and bottom of the bowl to make sure everything is evenly incorporated. Transfer the batter to a large bowl. Wash and dry whisk attachment and mixer bowl.

With the mixer on high, beat together the egg whites and salt until foamy, 1 to 2 minutes. With the mixer running, gradually add the remaining ½ cup of sugar. Continue to beat until stiff peaks form, about 5 minutes. Use a spatula to stir one third of egg white mixture into batter to lighten, then fold in remaining egg white mixture in 2 additions until combined.

Transfer the batter to the prepared pan and bake until the top of the cake is golden brown and a skewer inserted into the center comes out clean, about 40 minutes. Transfer to a wire rack and cool in the pan for 20 minutes. Run a knife around the edges of the cake to release the sides from the pan. Invert onto a plate, remove parchment, and then onto the rack right side up to cool completely.

Serve with whipped cream, berries, toasted nuts, honey, jam, or whatever you have in your kitchen.

HART'S

Pecan Sandies FOR MY MOM

My mom, Betty Keller, loved the Keebler pecan sandie. It was part of my childhood, and it's a flavor combination, vanilla and pecan, that I associate with her. There was always a bag of them in the cupboard. Or almost always. We were six kids, and we had our own cookies, but when we'd dispatched those, there would be that bag of Mom's pecan sandies. Sometimes, guiltily, we ate her cookies, one by one, until they were gone. Food is a powerful connector. Even the smallest thing—a cookie—can help us understand what we feel now while reminding us of what we once felt and who we've become versus who we were then. So much of who I am today is tied to my mom.

Recipe from *Bouchon Bakery* by Thomas Keller (Artisan Books). Copyright © 2012.

Thomas Keller, **BOUCHON BAKERY** • *Makes 1½ dozen cookies*

Ingredients

- 1 ¾ cups + 1 ½ teaspoons all-purpose flour
- ¾ cup coarsely chopped pecans
- 6 ounces unsalted butter, at room temperature
- ¾ cup + 1 ¾ teaspoons powdered sugar, plus more for dusting

Steps

Position the racks in the upper and lower thirds of the oven and preheat oven to 350°F. Line two sheet pans with Silpats or parchment paper.

Toss the flour and pecans together in a medium bowl.

Place the butter in the bowl of a stand mixer fitted with the paddle attachment and mix on medium-low speed until smooth. Add the ¾ cup plus 1¾ teaspoons powdered sugar and mix for about 2 minutes, until fluffy. Scrape down the sides and bottom of the bowl. Add the flour mixture and mix on low speed for about 30 seconds, until just combined. Scrape the bottom of the bowl to incorporate any dry ingredients that have settled there.

Divide the dough 1½-tablespoon portions, roll into balls, and arrange on the sheet pans, leaving about 1½ inches between them. Press the cookies into 2-inch disks.

Bake until pale golden brown, about 22 to 25 minutes, reversing the positions of the pans halfway through.

Set the pans on a cooling rack and cool for 5 to 10 minutes. Using a metal spatula, transfer the cookies to the rack to cool completely.

If desired, dust with powdered sugar.

Cookies can be stored in a covered container for up to 3 days.

BOUCHON BAKERY

Coconut Jam Bars

This recipe is a twist on Ovenly's Montego Bay Bars (date chocolate jam bars) and it happens to be very forgiving if you need to make substitutions based on what's in your pantry. I'm a lover of all things tropical, so I like to use guava and coconut, which is a favorite pairing of mine. It's the perfect balance of sweet and salty. However, any fruit jam you have at home will work well here in place of the guava paste.

Agatha Kulaga, **OVENLY** • *Makes 15 bars*

Ingredients

- 10 tablespoons unsalted butter, at room temperature, plus more for baking dish
- 1½ cups spelt or whole wheat flour
- 1¾ cups rolled oats
- 1 teaspoon sea salt
- ½ teaspoon baking soda
- ¾ cup unsweetened coconut flakes, divided
- 1 tablespoon extra-virgin olive oil
- 1 cup packed light or dark brown sugar
- 1 cup (8 ounces) fruit jam

Steps

Preheat oven to 350°F. Lightly coat a 9 x 13-inch baking dish with butter.

Whisk together flour, oats, salt, baking soda and ½ cup of coconut in a large bowl. Set aside.

In a stand mixer fitted with a paddle attachment (or using a hand mixer), beat the butter and olive oil with the brown sugar on medium speed until light and fluffy, about 3 minutes. Scrape down the sides of the bowl. Turn the mixer off, add the flour mixture, and mix on low speed until just combined. The mixture should be very crumbly and barely hold together when squeezed.

Press ¾ of dough mixture firmly into the bottom of prepared baking pan in an even layer (reserve ¼ of the mixture for the topping).

Spread jam in an even layer, covering the bottom crust.

Crumble the remaining ¼ of the dough mixture on top of the jam, covering the entirety of the jam. Sprinkle with reserved ¼ cup coconut, pressing gently to help stick.

Bake until lightly golden, 30 to 35 minutes. Let cool, then cut into 15, 3 x 2½ inch rectangles.

OVENLY

Salted Caramel Pudding

This classic dessert has graced the menu at West Village haunt Joseph Leonard for more than a decade.

James McDuffee, JOSEPH LEONARD • *Serves 6 to 8*

Ingredients

4 cups whole milk

1 cup sugar

3 large eggs

1/2 cup cornstarch

1 stick (1/2 cup) unsalted butter, cut into small pieces

1 teaspoon vanilla extract

1/2 teaspoon kosher salt

Softly whipped cream, flaky sea salt, and sugar cookies; for serving

Steps

Set a fine mesh sieve over a large heatproof bowl and set aside.

In a medium saucepan, bring milk to a simmer over medium-low heat, about 15 minutes. Reduce heat to low and keep milk warm while you make the caramel.

In a separate large pot, heat ¾ cup sugar over medium heat. Stir with a heatproof spatula and break up clumps until the sugar is dissolved, about 8 minutes. When the syrup comes to a boil, about 30 seconds, stop stirring. Swirl the mixture (but do not stir), until it turns a deep amber color, 1 to 2 minutes. Occasionally brush down the sides of the pot with a wet pastry brush to dissolve any crystals. Immediately add the hot milk to the caramel in a slow, steady stream (be careful, it will sputter), whisking constantly until the caramel is dissolved and mixture is smooth, 3 to 5 minutes. Remove from heat and set aside.

In a large bowl, combine the eggs, cornstarch, and 4 tablespoons sugar. Whisk gently to incorporate, then vigorously until the mixture is light in color and smooth and thick in texture, about 1 minute.

Whisking constantly, slowly pour about half of the hot caramel mixture into the egg mixture. Then, continuing to whisk, add egg mixture back into the saucepan. Cook the pudding mixture over medium-low heat, again whisking constantly, until the pudding is bubbling and thick enough to hold the marks of the whisk, 30 seconds to 1 minute.

Remove from heat and scrape the pudding into the sieve. Using a flexible spatula, press the pudding through the mesh into the bowl below (discard any solids left in the sieve). Whisk the butter into the pudding a piece at a time until smooth, then whisk in the vanilla and salt. Cover the pudding, pressing a piece of plastic directly onto the surface to prevent a skin from forming. Chill until cold, 2 to 3 hours. Spoon the chilled pudding into serving dishes and serve with whipped cream, flaky sea salt, and sugar cookies.

JOSEPH LEONARD

Lemon Ricotta Cake with Whipped Crème Fraîche

I love this cake because it's so versatile. It's perfect for dessert but also makes a quick, delicious breakfast with coffee in the morning.

Erin Shambura, **FAUSTO** • *Serves 8*

Ingredients

Cake
- Nonstick cooking spray
- 1½ cups all-purpose flour
- 2½ teaspoons baking powder
- ½ teaspoons baking soda
- 1 teaspoon Kosher salt
- 1½ sticks (¾ cup) unsalted butter, at room temperature
- 1½ cups sugar
- 1 pound fresh ricotta cheese, at room temperature
- 3 large eggs, at room temperature
- 2 tablespoons fresh lemon juice
- Finely grated zest of 1 lemon
- 1 teaspoon vanilla extract

Whipped Crème Fraîche
- 1 cup crème fraîche
- 1 cup heavy cream
- 1 tablespoon confectioners sugar

Steps

For cake: preheat oven to 350°F with rack in center position. Lightly coat bottom and sides of a 9-inch round cake pan with cooking spray, then line bottom with a round of parchment paper. Spray parchment paper.

In a medium bowl, whisk together flour, baking powder, baking soda, and salt to combine.

In the bowl of a stand mixer fitted with the paddle attachment, beat butter and sugar on medium-high speed until smooth, about 1 minute. Add ricotta and continue beating on medium-high speed, scraping down sides of bowl once or twice, until mixture is light and fluffy, about 5 minutes. Reduce mixer speed to medium. Add eggs one at a time, beating until each is well combined before adding the next, then beat in lemon juice, zest, and vanilla. Remove bowl from mixer, and using a spatula, fold in flour mixture in two additions.

Scrape batter into prepared pan and smooth out top with spatula. Bake until cake is deeply golden brown on sides, and top is puffed and no longer jiggling, 40 to 45 minutes. Let cool completely in pan on wire rack.

Meanwhile, make whipped crème fraîche: in the bowl of a stand mixer fitted with the whisk, beat crème fraîche, heavy cream and confectioners sugar on medium-low, increasing to medium-high until soft peaks form, 4 to 6 minutes. Transfer to a bowl, cover, and refrigerate until ready to serve. (Whipped crème fraîche is best immediately, but keeps, covered and chilled, for up to a day.)

Run a knife along cake edges to release sides, then invert cake onto wire rack. Remove parchment paper, then invert cake onto serving plate. Serve slices with whipped crème fraîche.

FAUSTO

Madeleines

Sometimes, it's not about making things complex and manicured, time-consuming and expensive. It's about how people feel about it. The simplest thing is the thing people remember the most. The madeleine is one of the things people crave—it doesn't matter how young or old you are. At Daniel, we often have people asking for extras to take home for their kids. So, universally, this is one of those cookies that just makes everyone happy.

Daniel Boulud, **DANIEL** • Makes 12 cookies

Ingredients

1 teaspoon baking powder

1/2 teaspoon Kosher salt

3/4 cup all-purpose flour, plus more for dusting

2 large eggs, at room temperature

1/4 cup + 2 tablespoon granulated sugar

1 teaspoon light brown sugar

1 teaspoon honey

1 lemon, zested

6 tablespoons unsalted butter, melted and cooled slightly

Nonstick vegetable oil spray

Powdered sugar, for dusting

Steps

Whisk baking powder, salt, and flour in a small bowl until combined.

Whisk eggs, granulated sugar, light brown sugar, honey, and lemon zest in a medium bowl until smooth, about 30 seconds. Whisk in dry ingredients until just incorporated. Whisk in melted butter until smooth, about 30 seconds. Transfer batter to a pastry bag or small resealable plastic bag and chill at least 1 hour, until thickened.

Preheat oven to 400°F. Lightly coat madeleine pan or mini muffin pan with nonstick vegetable oil spray and dust with flour, tapping out excess. Snip end (½ inch) off pastry bag or corner of resealable bag and pipe batter into each mold, filling each two-thirds full.

Bake madeleines until edges are golden brown and centers are puffed and lightly spring back when gently pressed and a toothpick, inserted, comes out clean, about 5 minutes for mini and 8 to 10 minutes for regular cookies.

Tap pan against counter to release madeleines. Using a sieve, dust with powdered sugar, and serve warm. Store cooled madeleines in an airtight container.

DANIEL

Acknowledgements

Serving New York is proof that amazing things happen when people roll up their sleeves and pitch in. This cookbook would not have become a reality without the support of the compassionate team below: family, friends, and colleagues generously donated their time, expertise, and resources.

To my dear friend and neighbor **Camilla Marcus**: You are an inspiration to us all. You inspired the idea for this book when you emerged as a leader during the early days of the pandemic. While everyone was still scrambling to figure out what to do, you were already forging ahead with big, impactful solutions. You are a ray of sunshine, even in the darkest times.

To **Bryan Fountain,** our incredibly talented designer: Thank you for believing in this book and its cause. Thank you for jumping in feet first and joining me on this wild ride. Without your big heart, hard work, and extraordinary talent, this book would not exist—and it certainly wouldn't look nearly as gorgeous.

To **Jordan Awan**: Thank you for creating the illustrations for the pages of this book. I'm so thankful to have had you on the team.

To **Allie Wist,** our photo editor: Thank you for spending so many late nights and early mornings (and during quarantine, no less!) tracking down and editing images. This project wouldn't be the same without your impeccable eye and talent.

Dawn Perry, thank you for your leadership, sage advice, and thoughtful edits. You were the first to throw your support and energy behind this project and I couldn't be more thankful for that. You are a true force in the food industry, and I'm honored to have worked with you.

To **Sasha Levine** and **Carey Polis,** two fiercely sharp editors, brilliant minds, and great connectors of people: Thank you for the long hours and hard work. This cookbook wouldn't have come together without your help.

Mindy Fox, I don't know what I would have done without you. Thank you for bringing your encyclopedic knowledge of cookbook writing and editing and incredible attention to detail to the pages of this book.

To the brilliant **Sarah Firshein,** thank you for lending your keen eye to this book. Your thoughtful edits and all-around guidance have been immeasurable. I feel incredibly lucky for your friendship and support.

To everyone who tested recipes, an exponentially harder task amid the coronavirus: You are all superheroes. You battled for the last bag of flour, endured long waits at grocery stores, and woke up at ungodly hours to grab Instacart delivery slots. I'm so grateful to **Lisa Nicklin, Shira Bocar, Alison Roman, Sara Tane, Mary Dodd, Erin Barnhart, Emma Rowe, Lauryn Tyrell, Olivia Anderson, Lisa Leonard-Lee, Laura Dozier, Lauren Young,** and **Sadie Guttman.**

To **Grace Elkus, Lauren Schaefer, Amiel Stanek, Claire Saffitz, Ananda Eidelstein, Farideh Sadeghin,** and **Mandy Naglich,** who tested and edited recipes to ensure home cooks of all skill levels can follow them. And **Rachel Tepper Paley,** thank you for your expert edits and all-around support of this project.

To **Nicole Schumann**: Thank you for responding to my manic emails and texts, and for being a dream to work with. As if you weren't already busy enough, you volunteered to recipe-test, and I can't thank you enough.

To the whole team at inHouse, thank you for giving this book a home and for championing this important cause.

Jamie Fass, you're the most on-top-of-it, organized person I know. Thank you for your support and enthusiasm.

Nikki Spilka and **Brean Antokal,** thank you for helping me make sure this book made plenty of noise. And to the journalists who wrote about it: Thank you for sharing the story and mission of this book with the world.

To my dear friends **Aaron Samuel Breslow, Jeremy Guttman, Ashley Roy, Corey Tuttle, Barrett Reeves,** and **Tanya Bhavnani**: I'm so incredibly lucky to have you in my life. Thank you for cooking up a storm and testing these recipes. And **Jessica Rothschild,** thank you for your expert advice and being one of my greatest cheerleaders throughout this process (and life in general).

To my family: Thank you for encouraging me throughout what felt, at first, like a crazy endeavor. You tested recipes (**Mom and Kacy**), you braved grocery stores (**Judy**), you sampled test dishes (**Dad, Steve, Billy, Carli, Maggie, Jake**), you gave me pep talks, and you made me believe that anything—even pulling together a cookbook in a month—is possible.

Special thanks to:

Noble Plateware
Brooklyn, NY
Sally Bowls
Hollywood Bowls
Brooklyn Bowls
Surreal Bowls

Helen Levi Ceramics
Queens, NY
Artist's Dinner Plate
Artist's Soup Bowl